FR

ABOU^r.

Amnon Danzig was born and raised in Israel, in a small community called a kibbutz.

Kibbutzim could, at that time, be characterised as "pure communism," in a positive sense: they embodied a direct form of democracy, with each working according to their ability, and each receiving according to their needs; this was almost utopian. The lessons Amnon learned from that period still influence his managerial thinking, especially regarding the advantages of small groups working in harmony and gaining from having a shared sense of ownership and significance for their work.

Over the last 25 years Amnon have worked in diverse senior roles, such as CFO, HR Director, Board Director, and Management Consultant.

The extensive experience Amnon has gained, combined with continuous reading and studying, has enabled him to develop unique frameworks and methods grounded in hands-on materials. Amnon have worked globally, in London, Singapore, the US, Canada, Western Africa, Spain, Russia and Israel.

His background allows Amnon to understand diverse human cultures and business environments.

In this book, "From Enigma to Paradigm," Amnon encapsulated the major themes which he have learned throughout his career.

1

Table of Contents

PREFACE

Dear Reader,

I have a few questions for you:

- ✓ How many times were you bothered by the direction your company is taking?
- ✓ How many times have you heard mumbo jumbo corporate strategy?
- ✓ How many times have consultants spewed jargon on how to steer your company, and you didn't have a clue what to do next?

Well, I have too, many times.

Which is why over the last two decades I've worked with managers all over the world to reveal a more fruitful and meaningful managerial life.

This is the journey that I shared with my esteemed colleagues: **From Enigma to Paradigm**.

The **Enigma** is the mystery of **management-in-action**; a few domains that we treat as silos, separate entities: accounting, economics, corporate finance, strategy, human behavior, managerial concepts, and more.

When people study management in school, they learn from each domain expert's best in class concepts. From these, the manager must form one body of knowledge, which is nearly impossible. Here, we fuse these management domains into one body of knowledge: the **Paradigm**.

Furthermore, as management is a co-evolving profession, each manager can make their own leap or **paradigm shift** to adapt their personal view of **management-in-action**.

Admittedly, there is nothing new here. The experienced manager "feels" various bodies of knowledge deep in his/her own healthy intuition. My role is to expose you to your own intuition, and fuse it with other bodies of knowledge that you may only have rough ideas about.

Hence, the reading will go pretty quickly in areas where you feel stronger, and slower in areas where you feel weaker.

In this book, I encapsulate my decades of international experience into three interrelated fields:

1. **Strategy**
   How your company can measure its **Competitive Advantage** in three dimensions: technology, brand, and finance.
2. **Finance**
   How your company can create **Shareholder Value** by taking into account its **stakeholders**.
3. **Management**
   How to make it happen.

This book was written as a journey:

I.   **Strategic dimension**

The most fundamental aspects of leading an organization. How to understand the **competitive advantage** of the product line within the appropriate markets. Then, what should be done to improve it, framed within two time horizons:

1. Operation Strategies (OS)
2. Growth Strategies (GS)

II. Financial dimension:

How to better understand the differences between the following bodies of knowledge:

a. Accounting
b. The economics of the company
c. Finance looking forward: how to deal with risk and uncertainty.

What are the merits one should earn from each body of knowledge?

III. Managerial dimension:

Taking into account the strategic and financial dimensions, what are the concepts and practices to manage the firm forward? Here, you will find practical examples to support you.

You can read this cover-to-cover, or choose chapters at your convenience to solve specific dilemmas.

One last word concerning the target audience for this journey **From Enigma to Paradigm**. My target audience is managers at manufacturing SMEs (Small-Medium Enterprises).

Why?

Simply because there is a vacuum in management literature for manufacturing SMEs. Most management literature comes from scholars and consultants that spin stories about best in class practices that have nothing to do with managerial life at manufacturing SMEs.

It is a well-known fact that SMEs are extremely significant for countries and their citizens; they employ a large portion of the population and are responsible for a sizeable share of many countries' economies.

However, I believe that other industries might draw some lessons from this journey as well. Why? Because product lines in specific regions behave like SMEs.

I hope you find your journey **From Enigma to Paradigm** worthwhile, both financially and in terms of your valuable time.

Sincerely yours,
Amnon Danzig

INTRODUCTION

While working with managers, I was astonished by the fact that even well-educated and well-read people were using professional expressions without grasping their true meaning.

This motivated me to explain even simple concepts in plain English. Because, in the end, what is the job of a consultant if not to set the stage for a **common language** among managers?
In this book I will do the same: explain each expression in simple words.

The job of the consultant is to set the stage for a common language among managers

---

I know it will seem rather ridiculous to seasoned managers, but I am sure you will appreciate it as you read along.

The structure of this book follows the rule of simplicity.
There are three parts:
- A. Strategy
- B. Finance
- C. Management

Each part consists of three chapters:
- 1. Intuition, Fundamentals and Principles

2. Managerial Implications
3. Tools & Practices

PART ONE: STRATEGY – THE COMPETITIVE ADVANTAGE MAP

Part One is dedicated to solving the enigma of a **competitive advantage** in four dimensions: technology, brand, distribution channels, and how to measure it (economically and financially). We will adhere to Michael Porter's explanation of the essence of "competitive advantage," and add two layers to it: measuring from an internal perspective (the economics of the firm) and then benchmarking it financially (other firms and the risk involved). This is a rather unique approach that will give managers a comprehensive understanding of the positioning of their firm, and inspire different methods to create growth strategies based on facts.

Chapter One: Intuition, Fundamentals and Principles
This chapter deals with the intuition of the matter: grasping the concepts in plain words.
We will also explore the theme of competitive advantage in-depth using several wide angle lenses: technology strengths, cost structure, offers to the end client, distribution channels, and brand strengths. The two polarities of "low cost" and "premium" will be treated with examples.

Chapter Two: Managerial Implications
In this chapter, we elaborate on the managerial implications of the competitive advantage. Taking into account the analysis in Chapter

One, we will explore the merits managers might expect to gain, and how to take them forward.

Chapter Three: Tools & Practices

In this chapter, we equip you with practices and tools that I've used quite extensively to assist managers in taking steps forward. Grasping the position of the firm in terms of competitive advantage is essential, but it only addresses the current competitive advantage. The wise manager should explore ways to gain sustainable competitive advantages; employing the appropriate tools and practices to continue to create sustainable competitive advantages over time. By doing so, the wise manager will materialize the strategic understanding he has already gained. These tools are applicable to any situation. However, applying them after you analyze your competitive advantage will bring much better results.

PART TWO: FINANCE – THE VALUE CREATION CONCEPT

In Part Two, we shed some light on the way firms create value. We start our journey with some well-established concepts that give the manager a glimpse into measuring value creation. We start with the differences between accounting frameworks, economic frameworks, and some financial frameworks. This will build the fundamentals to expand on the basic theme of value creation. Most of Part Two is based on the EVA (Economic Value Added) concept pioneered and developed by Joel Stern and Bennett Stewart while they worked at Stern Stewart & Co. I will take this a few steps further to ground some concepts we developed in Part One.

By the end of Part Two, you should understand the essence of the Value Creation Concept, and have a few ideas on how to measure it accurately.

Chapter Four: Intuition, Fundamentals & Principles

Some managers incorrectly believe that accounting, economics, and finance are the same body of knowledge. This leads boards to nominate CFOs with CPA (Certified Public Accountant) education. Bad mistake. I argue that boards should have a CFO with a wide ranging economic education, one who can serve the CEO on strategic matters. Not just a "bean counter," but someone to serve as the righthand person in strategic processes.

The fundamental differences between the accounting, economic, and finance sectors are detailed. These core differences inform the concept of EVA.

Building this framework allows us to elaborate on some managerial implications.

Chapter Five: Managerial Implications

Now, we are ready to fully grasp the outcomes the manager can gain from the Value Creation Concept. This is the core of the book: how managers can create value for shareholders while taking into account all of the stakeholders. This is the edge that a sustainable value creation company has over their peers. There are some dramatic insights that the manager should take away.

In the previous chapter, I described the EVA framework in brief. However, you should bear in mind that this is only the first step of the journey. The second step is to utilize it. The difference here is the outcome: it is not enough to implement a wonderful EVA framework without utilizing it within the managerial culture of the organization.

Consider that you live in Singapore and own a nice red Ferrari. Furthermore, that your experience of driving your Ferrari is similar to mine. Question: why do you want to own the Ferrari in the first place? Now, imagine that you own the Ferrari in Tuscany and your experience of driving it is comparable to Michael Schumacher's. This is the real difference between just implementing an EVA framework and actually knowing what to do with it. I think this is the missing link that we need to put in place together.

Chapter Six: Tools and Practices
In this chapter I equip managers with well-known tools that have been used across many firms. As mentioned before, these are based on the EVA framework.

PART THREE: MANAGEMENT – THE VALUE CREATION MINDSET

Let's continue to compare your red Ferrari in another example. Imagine you're an amateur cook who just bought a full-scale kitchen suited to a 3-star Michelin restaurant. You would probably prefer to sharpen your cooking skills by attending formal courses at the CIA (Culinary Institute of America) or Le Cordon Bleu. Let's face it: you can invest in best in class infrastructure without the knowledge to utilize it fully, essentially rendering your investment worthless.

I hope these two analogies are sufficient to convince you that best in class practices are worthless if you don't utilize them, adapting them to your organizational culture.

Furthermore, your organizational culture should meet the most urgent challenges of the 21st century, including how to compete simultaneously in four markets:

1. Customers
2. People (talent)
3. Business partners
4. Money

Let me elaborate:

1. Customers – You need to serve your clients with the right combination of cost structure and utilities, suited to them.
2. People – You need the right people to give you the edge in this battle.
3. Business partners – Looking at the competition as an ecosystem, you need to partner with the right entities suited to win the competition game for the end client.
4. Money – If you truly have success in the previous three markets, the money market (shares and debt) will be willing to offer you more than you need at lower costs.

The real conundrum is how to do it.

In Part Three, I suggest a few ways to do so while taking into account the previous two parts:

A. Part One: Strategy – The Competitive Advantage Map
B. Part Two: Finance – The Value Creation Concept

Chapter Seven: Intuition, Fundamentals and Principles

I propose two underlying assumptions:

I.   Workforce attitudes changed dramatically on the eve of the 21st century.
II. The current competitive landscape requires a new style of management to meet ongoing urgent needs.

In this chapter, I elaborate on the changes in these two fields and suggest the required mindset based on Parts One and Two.
The basic theme is to make the paradigm shift from Management 1.0 to Management 2.0.

> ➤ Management 1.0 was based on the scientific management style pioneered by Frederick Winslow Taylor. He laid out his ideas in his 1911 book *The Principles of Scientific Management*.
> ➤ Management 2.0 was coined by Gary Hamel. The two other scholars that contributed to this movement were Peter Drucker and Henry Mintzberg.

These two management mindsets represent the way we manage our firms. I can't wait to tell you the following story:
In the last two decades, I've given many lectures on management theories. In a few of them, the audience was rather delighted with themselves. I asked them where they would prefer to make their living, in a communist or capitalist regime. Sure, the most popular answer was a capitalist regime with all the slogans: laissez faire, the invisible hand, free will, entrepreneurship, sense of ownership, and the like. Quite convincing, right?
Taking the discussion forward, I then asked them how they described their firm's style of management: "Capitalism" or "Communism"? They seemed to be caught in a trap. I explained my view of the differences:

> ➤ Capitalism – The typical buzzwords the audience already provided are sufficient: laissez faire, the invisible hand, free will, entrepreneurship, sense of ownership, and the like.
> ➤ Communism – Central planning, rigid hierarchy, and the like.

The obvious question was, how do they explain this dichotomy? This will be elaborated at length. As such, our new management mindset is to:

> ✓ **Measure** correctly.

✓ **Compensate** accordingly.
✓ Lead to the right attitude and **sense of ownership.**
✓ And…**manage less!**

Chapter Eight: Managerial Implications

After we laid down the fundamentals and principles of the new management mindset, we are ready to disclose the implications: what is the role of the manager?

Furthermore, what outcomes should the company expect to achieve in terms of their competitiveness in the four market places we already defined:

- Customers
- People (talents)
- Business partners, and
- Money

The ultimate result of this new management mindset can be distilled as a "**prompt and comprehensive response.**"

Chapter Nine: Tools & Practices

In order to make the Value Creation Mindset actionable, we must equip you with a few tools. The journey you began will be realized by you and your colleagues who grasp the Value Creation Mindset. I must emphasize that each industry and each firm is unique. Hence, these tools and practices should be adapted and developed accordingly.

Chapter Ten: The Human Factor – Final Thoughts

We are approaching the final lap of our journey From Enigma to Paradigm. I would like to tell you a secret: we just studied the knowledge required to go From Enigma to Paradigm together. But in order to do this for real, we need to add the most powerful ingredient, the **human dimension**.

This last chapter is dedicated to the **human factor**. You do not want to miss it

Good luck on your new journey **From Enigma to Paradigm** adopting the **Strategic Value Creation Framework**.

PART ONE:

STRATEGY,

THE COMPETITIVE

ADVANTAGE MAP

CHAPTER ONE

INTUITION, FUNDAMENTALS

AND PRINCIPLES

Professor Michael Porter coined the expression Competitive Advantage in the early 1980s. He claimed there are only two polarities with which a company can create Competitive Advantage: low cost or premium.

THE TECHNOLOGY DIMENSION

Low cost refers to companies that can win the battle by producing within an extremely tight cost structure. Then they can sell at a price just slightly under their competitors, and save a nice margin for themselves.

Components of low costs can include: technology, energy, raw materials, workforce, infrastructure, taxes, interest rates and the like.

Premium is sometimes referred to mistakenly as brand value, but this is the end result. Here, premium refers to dynamically adapting to the customers' needs. I should emphasize that the company is working to be part of an ecosystem that serves specific clients in a precise way. This will be elaborated on later.

Premium refers to dynamically adapting to the customers' needs

---

The components of premium can include: technology, human capital, social capital, application engineering, distribution channels, value-added services, cooperation with other players in R&D and marketing, and the like.

The following figures are for a specific market, with a specific product line.

Figure 1-1 is the starting point:

Figure 1-1

The Competitive Advantage Map

Figure 1-2 is the second step:

Gather your senior and core people with extensive knowledge about your firm and your industry. Draw a circle that represents one of your competitors. The size of that circle should represent the size of that competitor related to your market.

Then spark a debate amongst your team to establish a common language about the way you all perceive the competitive landscape.

The aim: to create common language

It should be clear from the very beginning that there are no right or wrong judgements; rather, it is important to discover the way that each person understands the landscape. This discussion is extremely important for the firm. It should be re-emphasized that these judgements are intuitive and subjective.

Figure 1-2

The Competitive Advantage Map

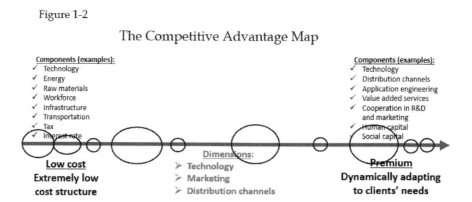

Now you have a clear, intuitive, and subjective view of the positioning of your company: a specific product line within a specific market.

You're ready to make your grand strategic choice: in which direction do you aim, low cost or premium? Once you decide, any managerial decision should be viewed through this lens of "low cost" or "premium." It should be clear that you will always work harder to achieve a lower cost structure. Bear in mind that this is not the strategic choice, it is the correct managerial attitude to widen your margin.

This question can serve as a springboard for any managerial decisions: ask yourself whether you are working toward "low cost" or "premium." Most companies do not have the capacity (intellectual or monetary) to work toward these two polarities at the same time.

THE ECONOMIC DIMENSION

Figure 1-3 adds the economic dimension, the internal performance results. The economic dimension adds a critical perspective for the profitability power of the company gained by creating competitive advantage. This is the end result of all efforts within the competitive landscape. The benchmark here is among the relevant competitors we judged previously in the technology and marketing dimensions.

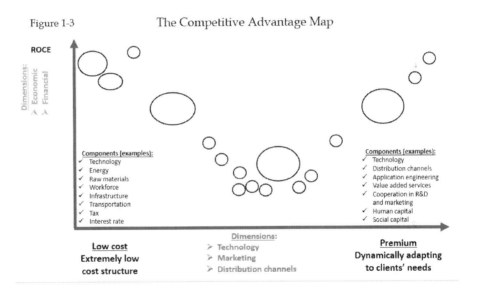

Figure 1-3   The Competitive Advantage Map

Now, we have a two-dimensional map reflecting the economic results of these companies' competitive advantages. In one glance, we can understand the competitive landscape.

Two-dimensional map reflecting the economic results of these companies' competitive advantages

We calculate the Return on Capital Employed (ROCE) for each company and plug it into the correct vertical dimension.

Let's review how to do this:

Assuming that we are dealing with publicly traded competitors, it should be rather easy to calculate their ROCE. Sure, it will be the company's and not the product line's ROCE, but for our strategic map it is sufficient to reflect the profitability power of the company. For private firms, we will have to make a few assumptions to estimate their profitability power.

ROCE is the overall profitably power since it reflects both the P&L (Profit & Loss) Statement and Balance Sheet Statement. In Part Two, I will elaborate on this quite extensively.

Just to give you a glimpse of the power of ROCE in terms of the real profitability benchmark:

Look at Table 1-1:

Table 1-1

$ in millions

	Company A	Company B
Revenue	1,000	1,000
Costs	750	850
Profit	250	150

Question: which company is better?

Sure, you will say Company A.

Now, take a look at Table 1-2:

Table 1-2

$ in millions

	Company A	Company B
Revenue	1,000	1,000
Costs	750	850
Profit	250	150
Capital Employed	2,500	1,000

Question: which company is better?

Hint:

Company A generated a profit of 250 by employing 2,500.

Company B generated a profit of 150 by employing only 1,000.

Now, what do you think?

Let's examine Table 1-3:

Table 1-3

$ in millions

	Company A	Company B	
Revenue	1,000	1,000	
Costs	750	850	
Profit	250	150	
Capital Employed	2,500	1,000	
Profit Margin	25%	15%	Profit / Revenue
ROCE	10%	15%	Profit / Capital Employed

It is easy to see that in terms of profitability, based only on a Profit & Loss Statement, Company A is better. But, if we prefer overall profitability power, taking into account the return for the capital employed, our conclusion is different: Company B utilizes its entire infrastructure much better.

This is just a brief explanation that will be developed further in Part Two.

Figure 1-4 adds the external dimension, the financial dimension, how much each company should profit in order to bear the risk involved.

The question is: how much earnings are "enough" to compensate investors for the risk in this particular industry? This methodology will be explained in-depth in Part Two. Here, I just provide an intuitive snapshot.

The RRR (Required Rate of Return) reflects the threshold for investor expectation. The RRR represents the minimum profitability power sufficient to compensate for the risk in the industry.

Hence, we divide Figure 1-4 into three regions:

1. Region I: The company creates value for its shareholders as the ROCE > RRR
2. Region II: The company is at "neutral," since ROCE = RRR. No value was created to compensate for the risk involved at this industry.
3. Region III: The company destroyed value, since ROCE < RRR. The risk is higher than the return.

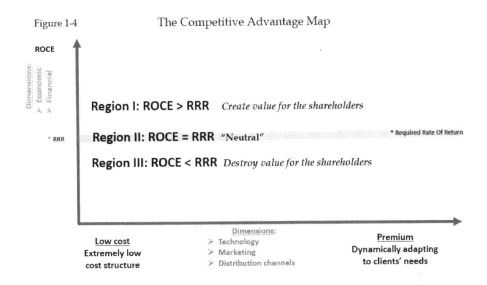

Figure 1-4   The Competitive Advantage Map

Region I: ROCE > RRR   *Create value for the shareholders*

Region II: ROCE = RRR "Neutral"   * Required Rate Of Return

Region III: ROCE < RRR *Destroy value for the shareholders*

Figure 1-5 puts everything together.

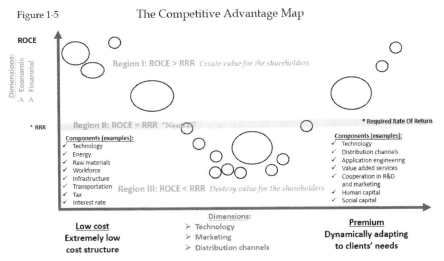

Figure 1-5   The Competitive Advantage Map

Looking at Figure 1-5 raises the following points:

➢ Region I: The companies that create value for shareholders are above the threshold simply because the Return on Capital Employed is above the Required Rate of Return. They have done this by choosing the appropriate strategy for them: either **"low cost"** or **"premium."**

➢ Region II: The companies that are in "idle" mode did not beat the threshold to compensate for the risk involved. They simply did not (or cannot) choose which type of strategy to adopt: **"low cost"** or **"premium."**

➢ Region III: Companies below the threshold are destroying value for shareholders because they could not choose or execute a winning strategy: either **"low cost"** or **"premium."**

In Chapter Four we will explore these financial aspects in-depth.

For now, it is sufficient to mention the 80/20 Principle, also known as the Pareto principle after the Italian Vilfredo Pareto who published it in the late 19th century. The 80/20 Principle can be seen at work in Figure 1-5, as well: around 80% of competitors are under the threshold. They simply cannot position themselves as either "low cost" or "premium." The other 20% differentiated themselves by adopting these "low cost" or "premium" value creation strategies.

This is an extremely important observation from the competitive advantage standpoint. The only way to create value for shareholders is to adopt the competitive advantage concept using The Competitive Advantage Map. Figure 1-6 emphasizes this.

Here you can see that 80% are struggling in The Ditch: they cannot escape without investing a huge amount of intellectual effort and money.

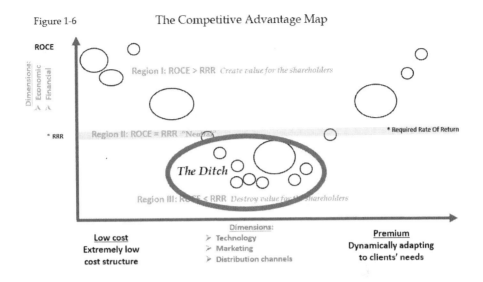

Figure 1-6   The Competitive Advantage Map

By drawing The Competitive Advantage Map, we now have a snapshot of how we perceive the current competitive landscape.

By drawing The Competitive Advantage Map, we now have a snapshot of how we perceive the current competitive landscape

---

The question now is, what are you going to do next? What are the avenues to win a sustainable competitive advantage?
This will be clarified over the following chapters.

CHAPTER TWO

MANAGERIAL IMPLICATIONS

Wrongly, many managers develop grand strategies full of jargon. I should emphasize that any good strategy starts from the bottom: the product line within a specific market. These are the building blocks for any good strategy. Strategy is not about big words.
Strategy is about understanding your competitive landscape and the unique offer with which you can equip your client. Period.

All other approaches are mumbo jumbo that cannot assist you in steering your company towards its critical competitive edge. Now, in order to appreciate the powers of the Competitive Advantage Map, it is essential to have a quick look at the history of strategic practices. Unconventionally, I will do this as a brief history of real strategy development practices in the manufacturing-industrial sectors over the last 100 years.

BRIEF HISTORY

I see it as three stages:
1. The Egocentric Approach
2. The Linear Approach
3. The Ecosystem Approach

The Egocentric Approach saw the industrial company as a standalone entity that should concentrate all of its effort internally.

Concentrate all of its effort internally

Once you are good at this, you win the strategic game.
Take a look at figure 2-1:

Figure 2-1

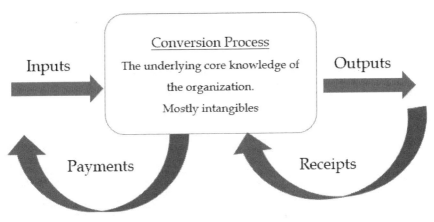

The Egocentric Approach

Inputs

Conversion Process
The underlying core knowledge of
the organization.
Mostly intangibles

Outputs

Payments

Receipts

"The Key to Success in the 20th Century"

Figure 2-1 illustrates all efforts within the firm: how to offer better products and services while improving constantly. In monetary terms, the spread between inputs and outputs encapsulates Profit & Loss terminology. The spread between payments and receipts encapsulates the results in cash flow terminology.
This strategy is extremely important nowadays. It gives managers the insight that only best-in-class products and services can win the game.

However, the weakness here is that the managers only look inward, leaving the big picture untouched: the competitive landscape.

In order to assist in differentiating between the three models, I will give you a litmus test.

Two questions:

1. Do you give your procurement manager a target of reducing the costs by x percent?
2. Do you give your marketing and sales director a target to increase the prices in y percent?

The lesson we draw from this is that you only prioritize creating value for your company. Period.

Figure 2-2 describes an enlargement of the Egocentric Approach to the **Linear Approach**:

Figure 2-2

The Linear Approach

Here the manager opens her scope and prioritizes the close environment: suppliers and clients. The manager wants to understand how his suppliers create value, including cost structure, competitive landscape, and the like. How can she cooperate with the supplier to provide a better offer to her own clients? As a mirror image of her relationship with suppliers, she looks to clients to understand their cost structure, their clients, and the like.

How to create value for the suppliers and clients

It does not mean that the manager stops looking inward. It means she develops a much wider understanding of both suppliers and clients. Furthermore, she would like to explore the suppliers of direct suppliers and the clients of direct clients. This gives her a better judgement of the competitive landscape.

Two litmus test questions here:
1. How can I create value for my clients?
2. How can I create value for my suppliers?

These questions lead to many strategic choices and activities.

It is worthwhile to note that the Linear Approach leads to the "vertical integration" M&A (Mergers and Acquisitions) concept:

- Backward integration = To buy the supplier.
- Forward integration = To buy the client.

The third approach borrows insights from evolutionary biology: The **Ecosystem Approach**.

Any organism that succeeds today built an entire network of relationships within its environment, called a cluster. Each partner within the cluster manages to contribute something that is essential to the other members of the cluster. As a result, they each get something essential from each another. Nobody tallies an income statement calculating how much they gain and lose. They just live and let live.

Figure 2-3

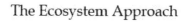

The Ecosystem Approach

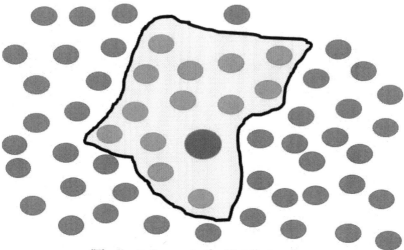

"The Key to Success in the 21st Century"

Think of it in 3-dimensions. In Figure 2-3 above, the blue circles (outside the fence) represent business partners. The green circles represent business partners within the cluster. The cluster is fenced just to show that they are the active members. There are no restrictions and regulatory practices to become a member within each cluster.

Any business partner that wants to be part of the cluster must demonstrate its capability to create a competitive advantage that justifies its membership. Like the behavior of organisms.

Any business partner that wants to be part of the cluster must demonstrate its capability to create a competitive advantage that justifies its membership. Like the behavior of organisms.

Here, The Competitive Advantage Map is essential to screen the competitive environment and assist the business partner to build the required strategic capabilities.

Three litmus test questions here:

1. How can I serve the desired cluster?
2. What kind of capabilities does the desired cluster need?
3. How can I create real sustainable value for the desired cluster?

These types of questions will steer the company to be an admired and sought-after business partner.

My guess is that the wise reader is raising her eyebrows at this point, waiting for me to address the following:

Within the cluster, the borders of companies become much more elusive and ill-defined. So, what is the purpose of the limited company in the first place? What should it aim for?

In 1937, young British scholar Ronald Coase was also bothered by the same question. His answer was published in his paper "The Nature of the Firm." He argued that companies exist because hierarchy "command and control" frequently beats markets. Companies exist because markets have limits where complex long-term planning and relationship are required. People created companies, said Coase, to avoid what he called "marketing costs." His argument was that the boundaries of the modern company were determined by the relative costs of market organization and hierarchical direction.[1]

For this paper, and another one, Coase won the 1991 Nobel Prize in Economics. Nowadays, there are so many types of companies that

[1] Ronald Coase: Nobel Prize winner who explored why companies exist. By John Kay. Financial Times, September 3, 2013

few of them can be described as Coase's "hollow company," or a company that does not own its manufacturing capabilities. This illustrates how companies that own their manufacturing capabilities create a competitive advantage that justifies their membership in their cluster.

IMPLICATION

Each firm must develop unique internal and external capabilities and relationships to create their edge and be known as a solid business partner within the cluster they desire.
While the Competitive Advantage Map can serve as one of the best tools to grasp your position in the competitive landscape, the next chapter will equip you with some simple, but extremely effective, tools and practices to take you forward.

Each firm must develop unique internal and external capabilities and relationships to create their edge and be known as a solid business partner within the cluster they desire

---

CHAPTER THREE

TOOLS & PRACTICES

This chapter is dedicated to tools and practices. Your journey will start from the most intuitive and simple, and lead to the more complicated and intellectually taxing. The reason for this is that we, as human beings, are more at ease dealing with intuition, and less at ease with long-term intellectual efforts.

Daniel Kahneman, in his book *Thinking, Fast and Slow*, describes how we think as two systems: (1) **System One**, and (2) **System Two**.

System One is the intuitive and easy way to manage multiple tasks. **System Two** can hardly manage one task at a time, and only for short spans of time. So, we will start by engaging with System One.

We begin with **two mapping systems** that enable us to better understand the competitive landscape.

We begin with two mapping systems that enable us to better understand the competitive landscape

---

Then we will move on to a tool to facilitate formal processes. This tool is a variant I developed from the Logical Framework method. Let's continue.

THE STRATEGIC VALUE MAP

The first mapping system is The Strategic Value Map. This map integrates two well-known tools:

1. SWOT Matrix (Strengths, Weaknesses, Opportunities and Threats) – deals with the firm's external and internal environments.
2. Radar Screen – a method for detecting the position and velocity of a distant object.

Figure 3-1

The Strategic Value Map

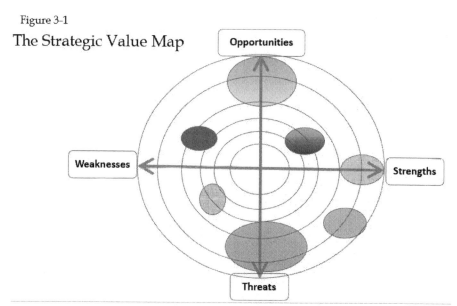

The idea here is to map a business initiative on a coffee shop napkin.

The idea here is to map a business initiative on a coffee shop napkin that create common language

---

Draw the map, and after five minutes you and your colleagues will create a common language to assess any new ideas.

The SWOT matrix is organized in a two-dimensional coordinate system. This visual description gives life to conventional SWOT wording. Note that:

1. The vertical dimension reflects the **external environment** of opportunities and threats.
2. The horizontal dimension reflects the **internal environment** of strengths and weaknesses.

The radar screen illustration addresses the uncertainty involved: likelihood and impact.

Here is how to complete your Strategic Value Map:

1. First layer:
   a. Position each item (project, event, business opportunity, business risk, and the like) on the map to best reflect your thinking in terms of:
      i. External environment:
         1. North – if it is an opportunity.
         2. South – if it is a threat.
      ii. Internal environment:
         1. Right – if it represents strengths you own.
         2. Left – if it represents your weaknesses.
2. Second layer:
   a. Likelihood: distance from the origin of the axes.
   b. Impact: the size of the bubble represents your intuition about the impact, if it should happen.

Now you have a full picture of your strategic landscape.

Of course, it is a static map that you should revisit on a regular basis.

The first layer provides you with a visual SWOT analysis.

The second layer provides you with a possibility and impact analysis.

The first layer provides you with a visual SWOT analysis.

The second layer provides you with a possibility and impact analysis.

This map enables you to make a quick prioritization analysis, and to determine a rapid action item plan.

It will give you intuitive insights into what should be done for each "bubble" you located on the map, and the interrelation between the "bubbles."

Let's take two extreme examples:

1. **Description**:

   The big bubble on the far north part of the map. This bubble represents a big opportunity that is far from possible. More than that, the firm does not own the capabilities to deal with this big opportunity.

   Prescription:

   If you feel it is a desirable opportunity, build the required capabilities. By doing so, you will move it to the right and enable yourself to tackle the opportunity with many more required resources.

2. **Description**:

   The big bubble on the far south part of the map. This bubble represents a big threat that is far from possible. More than that, the firm does not own the capabilities to deal with this big threat.

   Prescription:

If you feel it is a real threat, build the required capabilities to deal with it. By doing so, you will move it to the right and enable yourself to combat the threat with many more required resources.

Again, this is a quick, intuitive and qualitative tool that can be redeveloped and adapted for many business circumstances.

THE STRATEGIC VALUE NET

Now, we engage **System Two**, according to Daniel Kahneman's book *Thinking, Fast and Slow*. This second mapping system is The **Strategic Value Net** which draws lessons from the third stage in the evolution of the history of strategic practices described at length in Chapter Two, The **Ecosystem Approach**.

Any organism that succeeds in making its living today built an **entire network of relationships** within its environment. This network is called a **cluster**. Each partner within the cluster manages to contribute something essential to the other members of the cluster. As a result, they get something essential from one another.

Figure 2-3

The Ecosystem Approach

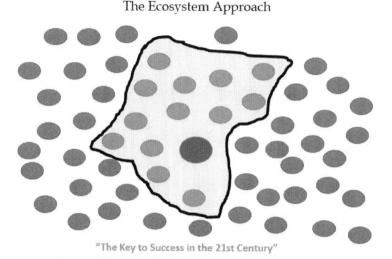

"The Key to Success in the 21st Century"

Think of it in three dimensions: the blue circles (outside the fence) represent business partners. The green circles represent business partners within the cluster. The cluster is fenced just to show they act as a team. There are no restrictions and regulatory practices to become a member of the cluster. Any business partner that wants to be part of the cluster must demonstrate its capabilities to create competitive advantages that justify its membership the cluster.

Any business partner that wants to be part of the cluster must demonstrate its capabilities to create competitive advantages that justify its membership the cluster.

Here is the roadmap to the **Ecosystem Approach**:
Develop a visual chart to describe as many business partners as you can think of that really take part in your cluster. See Figure 3-2 below.

Figure 3-2

The Strategic Value Net

An Industry Positioning and Strategic Support Tool

For illustrative purposes

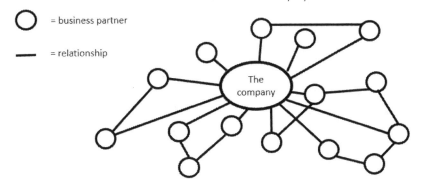

Prepared by Amnon Danzig & Janet Uy

In Figure 3-2, the circle represents business partners. The lines represent the relationship between two business partners. Then, for each business partner create a Crystallized Company Sheet as in Figure 3-3 below and connect it to Figure 3-2 via hyperlink. The Crystallized Company Sheet is for each market in terms of geography.

Figure 3-3

Crystallized Company Sheet

For illustrative purposes

- Revenue segmentation:
  - Market (in geographic terms)
    - Industry A
    - Industry B
    - Industry C

- Sources of competitive advantage:
  - Market (in geographic terms)
    - Industry A
      - ✓ Premium – dynamic adaptation for niche markets
      - ✓ Low cost structure
    - Industry B
      - ✓ Premium – dynamic adaptation for niche markets
      - ✓ Low cost structure
    - Industry C
      - ✓ Premium – dynamic adaptation for niche markets
      - ✓ Low cost structure

For each line representing the relationship between two business partners, create a Crystallized Relationship Sheet (see Figure 3-4 below) and connected it to Figure 3-2 via hyperlink. The relationship should be defined here on a macro level, between companies.

Figure 3-4

Crystallized Relationship Sheet

For illustrative purposes

- Human interactions
  - Major meetings
  - Exchanges of emails
  - Others
- Competition
  - ...
  - ...
  - ...

- Cooperation
  - ...
  - ...
  - ...
- Mutually developing:
  - Products
  - Services
  - Technology
  - Distribution channels
  - Others

Hence, Figure 3-2 articulates the cluster's landscape in two layers:
1. Each business partner with his own Crystallized Company Sheet.
2. Each relationship between two business partners with a Crystallized Relationship Sheet.

A hyperlink connects each circle or line to the appropriate doc. These docs should be simple to create and make it easy to grasp the information. This will give you a wide picture of the competitive landscape for a specific cluster.

The preparation should be done by a strategic analyst who gathers the info from your core people and external sources.

You can then revisit your specific Competitive Advantage Map, described in Chapter One, to build your roadmap for achieving a competitive edge within your cluster.

44

Now you are ready to deploy the roadmap: the formal planning.

ROADMAP FOR FORMAL PLANNING

The following roadmap for formal processes is a variant I developed from The Logical Framework.
As I warned you, this planning requires considerable intellectual efforts from you and your team.

This planning requires considerable intellectual efforts from you and your team

---

However, by doing this planning, you will gain a creative and robust roadmap. Promise.

Go over Figure 3-5 to crystallize the roadmap for your integration within your desired cluster.
As Winston Churchill said, "Plans are of little importance, but planning is essential."

Figure 3-5

Strategic Positioning

Vision Statement *Why do we exist?*

Differentiation Method:
✓ Premium – dynamically adapting to clients' needs
✓ Low cost – extremely low cost structure

	Short Description	Current Capabilities	New Desired Capabilities	Internal Assumptions	External Assumptions
Mission *Why?*					
Outputs *Results*					
Inputs *The Plan*					

The logic here is counterintuitive: start from the big picture of the end results and perform reverse engineering to the working plan.

The logic here is counterintuitive: start from the big picture of the end results and perform reverse engineering to the working plan

---

Most humans find it easier to go the other way around, from the working plan to the results. Hence, thinking strategically requires us to leapfrog to the way you would like to see yourself as part of the cluster. What can we contribute to the cluster? Therefore, we go from top to bottom.

What can we contribute to the cluster?

Each cell in Figure 3-5 requires a one-page description behind it.

Let's start:

1. **Vision Statement** – in a few paragraphs, describe the reason your company exists. It takes some time and a good debate to make sure the team is on the same page. Without it, you cannot go forward.

2. **Differentiation method**: here you just decide which method you would like to use: **premium** or **low cost**. This decision will determine the entire strategy. So make sure your decision is articulated wisely.

   The rows, again, proceed counter-intuitively.

3. **Mission** – elaborate in each cell the "why" questions:

   a. **Short description** – what is the interrelated logic between the vision and the mission? What do you expect to gain from it?

   b. **Current capabilities** – what are the capabilities the firm currently owns that might fulfill the mission? Capabilities can be in terms of infrastructure, R&D, technology, marketing, distribution channels, logistics, manufacturing, and the like. Here you must be very precise. No big buzzwords. Just exactly what you own.

   c. **New, desired capabilities** – capabilities you need to accomplish your mission. This list is similar to the current capabilities, but here you can consider in-house capabilities and/or subcontractors.

   d. **Internal and external assumptions** are the very basis of risk protocol. Here, you prepare the soil for your entire risk protocol, which is the most important component of any good program. You may prefer to be assisted by Figure 3-1: The Strategic Value Map. At the end of this chapter, I will equip you with a simple methodology to make sure you prepared your internal and external assumptions properly.

    i. **Internal assumptions** – what are the causes from within that could destroy the success of the project? These causes are under your influence. You must identify very specific causes. Most of the time, the corporate culture and the participation atmosphere within the organization play a major role.

    ii. **External assumptions** – what are the causes not under your influence that might destroy the program? Again, you must be very specific.

4. **Outputs** (results) – go over the same columns, but elaborate from the "outputs" perspective.

5. **Inputs** (the plan) – again, go over the same columns, but from the "to-do checklist" perspective.

    The columns' short descriptions and current and desired capabilities are pretty straightforward: one time you elaborate it from the "results" perspective and then from the "to-do-list" perspective.

    The internal and external assumptions columns are another story altogether:

    At the intersection of internal assumptions and outputs, you write the negative outcomes IF they happen. At the intersection with inputs, you write what should be done to avoid it, in general terms.

This should be the right springboard for a comprehensive risk program.

Elaborate Figure 3-5 in 15 separate pages that hyperlink to the associated cells. Each page covers one cell.

At the end of this effort, you should gain a comprehensive and mutual understanding of your strategy per specific product line within a specific niche market.

Now, you initiate the plan that articulates the "**How**" and "**What**" in order to be a fair business partner within your cluster.

Note: Walking through Figure 3-5 will give you nice insights concerning first order consequences: the desired outputs. The immediate results.

However, each decision also brings second order consequences that you did not think of in advance. Surely, third and fourth order consequences will erupt as well. My toolbox has other tools that can help you take into consideration consequences you did not predict.

As a glimpse, I advise you to take a wide-scoped to reframe the situation a couple of times and look into the future with counterintuitive thinking. Pre-mortem is the first tool at hand.

Wrap up:
I think that the best way to wrap up this chapter is by assisting you with the following tool: Pre-mortem.

PRE-MORTEM

Pre-mortem is a tool that utilizes the **prospective hindsight** concept.
Prospective Hindsight is a way to look forward by looking backward. You assume you have already reached the point of a few years from now, and try to figure out why certain things happened.

Prospective Hindsight is a way to look forward by looking backward

---

Pre-mortem is a close cousin of **postmortem**. Postmortem is used by medical doctors to understand why they failed after the patient passes away.

Gary Klein took the **postmortem** one step further and adapted it to managerial situations, hence the Pre-mortem methodology. Daniel Kahneman made it popular in his book *Thinking, Fast and Slow*.

My version of Pre-mortem is the following.

After you finalize your project plan, and everything is ready for kick-off, gather your management team and all the core people that were part of the knowledge base of the project. Do it on Friday evening, just one hour before the end of the workday.

Clear mobiles, laptops and other disturbing machines from the room.

Each person gets: one bottle of beer, a sheet of paper, and a pencil.

Each person gets: one bottle of beer, a sheet of paper, and a pencil.

Here is your pitch:

"Ladies and gentlemen, today is (give a date three years from now). The project has failed. Furthermore, it puts our company at risk. Period.

Now you have a budget of seven minutes and one bottle of beer.

The budget: seven minutes and one bottle of beer

Please, write the chronology of this failure; all the things that caused this dramatic failure. MOVE."

After seven minutes, gather the papers and thank the participants. You then take the papers and read them carefully at home. Read and reread until you fully expose yourself to the new insights your colleagues have shared with you.

At a glance, this encapsulates the entire body of knowledge of the project's shortcomings and disadvantages: what are the causes of this dramatic failure?

The entire body of knowledge of the project's shortcomings and disadvantages

---

Next Monday morning, you gather the same group: a sheet of paper and pencil for each participant. No beer…

Ask them to articulate the program, taking into account what they wrote on Friday evening. Give them one hour. Collect the papers and thank them.

Now you have a fine springboard to re-examine the project.

The reason to do it is pretty simple: while preparing new projects under your strong leadership, all the doubts, critics, annoying facts and unpopular standpoints are moved to the side.

Your team can develop group thinking, which is very dangerous when preparing the knowledge base for the new project. In Pre-mortem you give a "license" for this negativism about the project, or parts of it.

In Pre-mortem you give a "license" for this negativism about the project, or parts of it.

Daniel Kahneman said that executives find this extremely beneficial to them.

In this chapter, I equipped you with some basic tools for your journey to create an appropriate strategy to become a respected business partner in the cluster you choose.

Good luck!

PART TWO:

FINANCE,

THE VALUE CREATION

CONCEPT

CHAPTER FOUR

INTUITION, FUNDAMENTALS

AND PRINCIPLES

This book is the ultimate intersection of strategy, corporate finance, and management. It serves as the missing link for manufacturing SMEs in particular.

I wrote this book for managers. It is a How To book, not an academic book. It should serve you, the reader, as a firsthand assistant on your journey to create sustainable value.

This book is the ultimate intersection of strategy, corporate finance, and management

---

I must warn you that this chapter is lengthy and at times quite difficult to comprehend. If you are familiar with corporate finance or understand the EVA[2] (Economic Value Added) concept, you will find this chapter readable. If not, read it twice.

If you understand just 60% of the concept, fair enough. Chapter Five deals with managerial implications, and Chapter Six offers some tools and practices. After you finish reading the entirety of Part Two (chapters 4-6) you gain a basic understanding of the Value Creation Concept. For your convenience, at the end of this

---

[2] Pioneered by Joel Stern. *Stern Stewart & Co.*, the consultancy firm populated it.

chapter I provide you with a website that can sharpen both your understanding and technical skills. Stay tuned.

Before we lay out the fundamentals of value creation, let me draw a few distinctions within the sphere of the financial landscape. There are three separate, but interlinked, domains:

1. The accounting domain
2. The economic domain
3. The finance domain

Note: For the sake of simplicity we will take many shortcuts. The curious reader can compensate herself with the website mentioned at the end of this chapter.

* * *

THE ACCOUNTING DOMAIN

- ➢ Goal:
  - o To work with standards that enable comparison between firms.
- ➢ Characteristics:
  - o Dealing with the past.
  - o Heavy regulations from state and international bodies.
  - o Robust framework.
- ➢ Features:
  - o Three interlinking statements give a comprehensive picture of the company:

1. **Balance sheet statement** describes two points in time. These are snapshots of assets the company owns and the way it is financed. There are two statements that analyze the causes of the differences between these two snapshots:

2. **Profit and Loss statement** (P&L). The beauty of the P&L statement is its ability to analyze the differences between the balance sheet snapshots from the **profitability** standpoint: **revenue** and its **cost structure**.

The beauty of the P&L statement is its ability to analyze the differences between the balance sheet snapshots from the profitability standpoint: revenue and its cost structure.

Revenue is defined as a good or service delivered to the responsibility of the customer. It is documented by an invoice. Therefore, the aggregate of the invoices is typically coined as revenue.

Cost is defined by **expense** that **generates** the **revenue**. This is the well-known definition of the "**matching principle**."

By using the "**matching principle**" extensively, accountants tend to draw a **causation relationship** between **revenues** and **costs**. This enables them to figure out the **profitability structure** of the firm. Though accountants went just halfway with the "matching principle," distorting measurements and, consequently, distorting the management of the firm.

I will return to this point when we talk about the economic domain later on in this chapter.

The "matching principle" enable to show causation relationship between revenues and costs: the profitability structure of the firm

---

3. **The cash flow statement** analyzes differences between the two snapshots in the balance sheet from the cash streams perspective: in and out.
   The aim of the cash flow statement is to shed some light on the **health** of the **company**. Here we can make the analogy between our body and the firm: money and blood. In the Bible you can find the Hebrew word *damim*, meaning "blood" and… money! It is not a coincidence that a company losing money is referred to as "bleeding" or "hemorrhaging" cash.

Figure 4-1

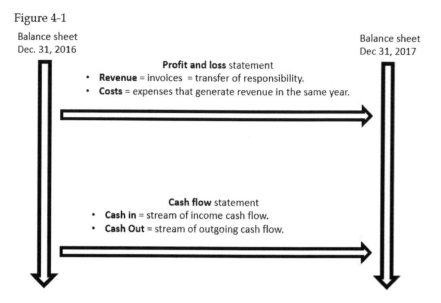

Balance sheet
Dec. 31, 2016

Balance sheet
Dec 31, 2017

Profit and loss statement
- **Revenue** = invoices = transfer of responsibility.
- **Costs** = expenses that generate revenue in the same year.

Cash flow statement
- **Cash in** = stream of income cash flow.
- **Cash Out** = stream of outgoing cash flow.

Summary:

The accounting domain gives a good picture of the history of the firm from the numeric standpoint. It is a robust framework that has regulators in charge of it. Furthermore, external auditors check that the company complies with the rules.

However, it would be a huge mistake if managers tried to make decisions using the accounting framework. Though it gives a solid springboard to migrate from the **accounting framework** to **the economic framework.**

However, it would be a huge mistake if managers tried to make decisions using the accounting framework

---

THE ECONOMIC DOMAIN

- ➢ Goal:
    - o To give managers tools to make wise decisions.
- ➢ Characteristics:
    - o Dealing with the past.
    - o Flexible to reflect the past via economic lenses.
    - o Not robust. The economist will have to make her best judgement call by making the leap from the **accounting framework** to the **economic framework**.
- ➢ Features:
    - o Two interlinking statements give a comprehensive picture of the company:
        1. **Economic Profit and Loss statement**. The economic structure of revenue and costs.
        2. **Economic balance sheet statement**. The economic structure of the capital employed, and the way it was financed.

Economic Profit and Loss statement:

Accountants went just halfway when using the "matching principle." The Profit and Loss statement should reflect the cause and effect phenomenon:

Accountants went just halfway when using the "matching principle."

Expense is a **cost** only if it creates revenue in the timespan of less than one year.

Expense is an **investment** only if it creates a revenue in the timespan of more than one year. Essentially, it is a multiyear effect. Any expense that has an effect **within one year** should be recorded as a **cost**.

Any expense that has a **multiyear effect** is an **investment** and should be recorded as fixed assets.

Machinery and buildings are the most obvious examples of investments. Accountants call them **tangible assets**.

Economists claim that **capitalized intangibles** influence the company's performance on a multiyear basis.

Economists claim that capitalized intangibles influence the company's performance on a multiyear basis.

For example, **expenses** like Research and Development (R&D), marketing efforts, human capital, and the like are described by accountants as **intangible**. Any manager understands that these items will influence the future of her company. Yet accountants insist on treating them as costs.

The **managerial outcome** is obvious: there are not enough efforts in R&D, marketing, and other expenses that truly influence the future of the company. The managers would like to have a nicer P&L statement. And hence, the wise manager will give all kind of excuses as to why she is not investing in the future of the company by investing in the right R&D and marketing efforts.

Here you can see that the accountant did not go the extra mile to make sure the manager's behavior is rational for the future of the company. He does not "walk the talk."

The economic Profit and Loss statement solves this using two principles:
1. The matching principle, and
2. Judgement calls.

I will refer to the mechanics of these in Chapter Six.

The accountant did not go the extra mile to make sure the manager's behavior is rational for the future of the company.

The most striking difference between accountants and economists is the **cost of capital**.

For example, let's assume there are two firms:
1. Company A - fully leveraged
2. Company B - financed with equity. No debts.

Table 4-1

$ in millions

	Company A	Company B
Revenue	1,000	1,000
Operation costs	750	750
Interest costs	100	–
Profit	150	250

Notes:		
Financed with debt	V	
Financed with equity		V

Questions:

- Can you justify the difference in profit between companies A and B?
- How about the matching principle that defines a cost as an expense that generates the revenue?

Remember that all assets that took part in generating the revenue should be part of the costs.

Economists believe it is unimportant how the company financed its assets. What is important is that the company's assets that were part of the revenue generation are taxed appropriately.

Economists believe it is unimportant how the company financed its assets

---

If one is willing to understand the cost structure of the company, one must take into account the opportunity cost of using the shareholders' funds, from the shareholders' perspective.

Let's elaborate on this:

The owners can invest in another company with the same risk profile as their own. The risk associated with this similar company in the same industry represents the opportunity cost for the owner. The interest rate reflects the risk. (We will deal with this later on in this chapter).

The traditional P&L takes into consideration the way the company finances its capital employed (I will elaborate on this in a few minutes). The economist's view is different: it is not important how the company finances its operations. The managers have the responsibility to track how much capital they use in order to generate revenue. This way, the managers see the costs not only in terms of the typical P&L, but also the costs of holding infrastructure and other assets like inventory and accounts receivable (credit that the company gave its customers).

The economist's view is that managers should be accountable for the entire cost of doing business. And this includes the cost of using the capital employed.

The economist's view is that managers should be accountable for the entire cost of doing business. And this includes the cost of using the capital employed

---

Economic balance sheet

The accountants see the **capital employed** as the total assets minus current liabilities. Or, equivalently, fixed assets plus working capital. Whereas the economic view is aligned with the "matching principle": take into account only the true operational assets that generate the revenue. Here I will paint an abstract picture, and in Chapter Six I will elaborate on the mechanics of it.

The balance sheet statement has two major components: **assets** and **liabilities**.

The **assets** are items that belong to the company.

The **liabilities** are the way the assets were financed.

The basic illustration of a balance sheet is:

Figure 4-2

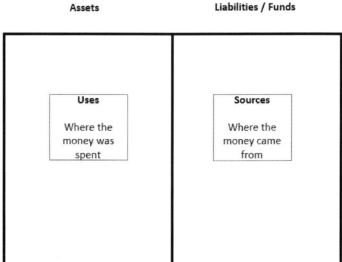

Assets are divided into two main groups:
1. **Fixed assets** – assets that have been generating revenue for multiple years.
2. **Current assets** – assets that are generating revenue in the current year.

Liabilities are divided into two main groups:
1. **Long-term liabilities** – equity (the shareholders' investment) plus long-term debt. Long-term debt should be paid out during a period that is longer than one year.
2. **Short-term liabilities** – liabilities that should be paid out during the current year.

The basic differences between how accountants and economists observe the balance sheet statement can be described by the following examples.

Capital employed are the true assets that generate revenue: **fixed assets** plus **working capital.**

Capital employed are the true assets that generate revenue: fixed assets plus working capital

---

Fixed assets generate revenue in multiyear patterns. These include tangible assets ("items you can touch") like buildings and machinery, as well as **capitalized intangibles.**

Capitalized intangibles are items you cannot touch such as human capital, R&D, marketing efforts, and the like. Accountants see these costs and put them in the P&L statement. This is where they are going only halfway with the "**matching principle.**"

Firstly, there is no doubt that these types of expenses won't generate revenue only within one year. Furthermore, putting intangibles in the P&L statement reduces the "bottom line" (the profitability of the firm) and hence discourages managers from making these efforts. By doing so, accountants neglect the value creation of the firm over a longer horizon. Here you can see the essential differences between accountants and economists: how to measure performance in order to influence managers to make better decisions for the value creation of the firm. Not merely a short-termism approach for annual profitability.

The essential differences between accountants and economists: how to measure performance in order to influence managers to make better decisions for the value creation of the firm

---

In general, management is in a constant struggle, the trade-off of inputs for better outcome. The Value Creation Mindset is all about thinking and operating for the long-term future of the company. **Working capital** is observed by accountants as **current assets** minus **current liabilities**.

Current assets are defined as assets that will generate revenue or cash in one year.

Current liabilities are composed of short-term debt to suppliers, and short-term debt to loan providers.

Accountants see it as "one package", insisting that the **current liabilities** include the debt that carries interest costs and **non-interest-bearing current liabilities** (**NIBCLE**).

Economists make sharp distinctions between debts that carry interest payments and debts to service providers that bring credit to the company with (officially) no costs.

Hence, for the economist, working capital is **current assets**, minus **non-interest-bearing current liabilities** (**NIBCL**).

By doing so, management is encouraged to increase the credit the firm got from their suppliers.

To sum it up:

The accountant's view is that the company's **capital employed** consists of fixed assets (without the intangible) plus working capital (current assets minus all current liabilities).

The economist's view is that the company's **capital employed** consists of fixed assets (including the intangible) plus working capital (current assets minus non-interest-bearing current liability). This way, the measurement system encourages the managers to take the long-term view by making wise decisions.

Here you can see it in charts:

Figure 4-3

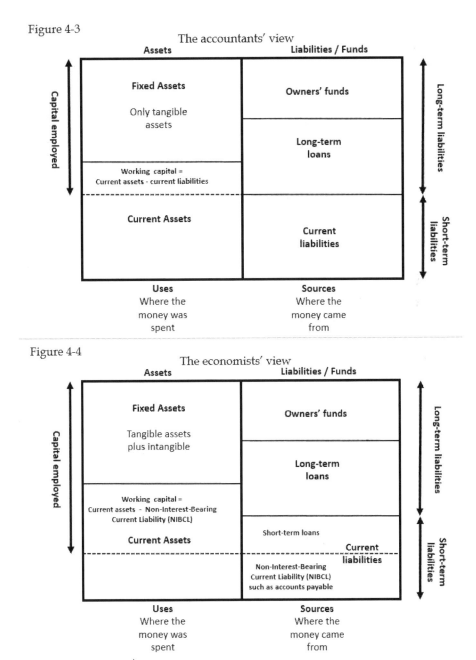

The accountants' view

The economists' view

I am sure that managers that work within the manufacturing SMEs sector will see it as a revolutionary approach. I know it.

Experienced managers see the accounting domain as the springboard to manage the firm. If the CFO (Chief Financial Officer) earns her education within the accounting sphere, well, "Houston, we have a problem." You as a manager will not get the right tools to make wise decisions.

My dear reader, I would like to tell you a secret: the economic domain is not new. Not at all. Any student who learns corporate finance is well aware of it.

Yes, the **measurement** of **value creation** is not new. Alfred Marshall wrote, "what remains of the owner's profits after deducting interest on his capital at the current rate, may be called his earnings of undertaking or management."[3] Marshall emphasized that **economic profit** must take into account the **opportunity costs** of the **capital employed** in the business.

Peter Drucker (1909-2005) said during a discussion with Fortune's editor that "…And there is no profit unless you earn the cost of capital. Alfred Marshall said that in 1896, Peter Drucker said that in 1954 and in 1973, and now EVA (Economic Value Added) has systematized this idea, thank God."[4]

This is the first step to start implementing your **Value Creation Mindset**.

In summary:

The **economic domain** generates two important measures, and one ratio:

---

[3] Alfred Marshall (1842-1924), Principles of Economics, 1890, Vol. 1. Page 142.

[4] Peter Drucker Takes The Long View. The original management guru shares his vision of the future with FORTUNE's Brent Schlender. By Brent Schlender; Peter Drucker, Reporter Associate Lixandra Urresta
September 28, 1998

1. Economic profit (EVA – Economic Value Added)
2. Economic Capital Employed
3. ROCE – Return on Capital Employed

I will refer to each of these in Chapter Six. For now, I will give you just a taste of the ROCE.

Calculation:

ROCE = NOPAT* / Economic Capital Employed**

+ EBIT (Earnings Before Interest and Tax)

+ Tax (add the tax)

+ Intangible expenses (add back: R&D, Marketing, Human Resources, and the like)

= NOPAT* (Net Operating Profit After Tax)

+ Fixed assets = Tangible assets + capitalized intangibles (R&D, Marketing, Human Resources, and the like)

+ Working Capital = **Current assets** minus **non-interest-bearing current liability**

= Economic Working Capital**

The ROCE is the profitability ratio we will need at the end of this chapter.

THE FINANCE DOMAIN

➤ Goals:
  o Dealing with the future.

- o Give managers tools to make wise decisions about the future.
- ➤ Characteristics:
  - o Quantify the risk associated with an uncertain future.
  - o Flexible by working hand-in-hand with economic lenses.
  - o Not robust. The finance person makes her best judgement call by giving recommendations for the future activities of the firm.
- ➤ Features:
  - o Equip managers with tools to deal with the future.
  - o Make them aware of the risk phenomenon.
  - o Understand risk and how to measure it.
  - o The return phenomenon.
  - o The relationship of return and risk.
  - o Human phenomenon. The agency theory (see Chapter Six).

THEORY AND PRACTICE

It is quite a disturbing fact that any graduate of an MBA program has studied corporate finance in-depth, but by the time she enters the workforce she does not have the capacity to implement the theories she has studied. As a consultant, I heard too many times that "this is just a theory. Let's go to real life."
Albert Einstein said, "It is the theory which decides what can be observed."

Albert Einstein said, "It is the theory which decides what can be observed."

Einstein's sentence should be read twice: it will give a sense of the importance of good theory. Good theory is not about "true" or "false." Good theory is all about what gives you the opportunity to understand, explain, and hence, predict.

Too many managers are bounded by the seat-of-the-pants trap. Good managers learn from experience how to cope with day-to-day routine, the "**how**" practices. The best managers must add another layer: learn the theory behind it to prepare for new challenges. The best managers learn the "**why**," and then develop their own "**how**" based on theory and their own experience. This is exactly what I am doing in this book: mapping the best and most applicable theories in the most practical ways.

THE PROBLEM WITH THE FUTURE

So, let's begin with your prime challenge as a manager: how the near and far future will influence the company's performance. How to spot opportunities and threats in the coming future.

Well, there is no crystal ball, yet, but the wise manager should equip herself with various frameworks to deal with these types of uncertainties. In Part One I gave you few strategic models to cope with an uncertain future. Here, in Part Two, I will shed some light on financial tools that assist you in quantifying uncertainty with few risk measures.

Let's start with some definitions that will help us develop our understanding:

➢ **Future** – a period of time that is to come.

➢ **Uncertainty** – "we **don't know** that we **don't know**": cannot be predicted.

➢ **Risk** – "we **know** that we **don't know**": quantify the "don't know" with statistical tools. In corporate finance terminology, risk is NOT about "**good**" or "**bad**." It is the state of mind that "we know that we don't know." Hence, we quantify it with statistical tools like variance. Trying to reflect past events gives a measure that elaborates the differences between what **is expected**, and what actually **happened**. That measure suggests what the variance should be for the future based on past events.

➢ **Measuring Risk** – as we agreed before, risk in finance is not about "**good**" or "**bad**," it is about variance. Now, we are taking one step forward to measure. The measure is called: beta (β). In finance, the **beta** (β or **beta coefficient**) of an investment indicates whether the investment is more or less volatile than the market as a whole. Beta is a measure of the risk arising from exposure to general market movements, as opposed to idiosyncratic factors. The market portfolio of all investable assets has a beta of exactly 1.[5]

➢ Let's assume that the S&P 500 represents the entire market. In finance it is common to say that the S&P 500 serves as a good proxy for the entire market. The beta of the S&P 500 is "1" (index-wise). Any single investment **greater** than "1" implies

---

[5] https://en.wikipedia.org/wiki/Beta_(finance)

that the volatility of this particular investment is **higher** than the S&P 500. Any single investment **smaller** than "1" implies that the volatility of this particular investment is **lower** than the S&P 500.

Let's illustrate what you can expect to gain by looking at the beta number.

Suppose the entire market is flowering and expanding. So, while the S&P 500 grew by "1" (index-wise) the industry (or firm) that has a beta of 1.5 will grow by 1.5 times. If another industry has a beta of 0.8, it will grow by 0.8 of the market.

In declining and contracting market conditions, when the S&P 500 shrinks by "1" (index-wise) the industry that has a beta of 1.5 will shrink 1.5 times. If the industry has beta of 0.8 it will shrink only 0.8 times. Now, we can grasp that the beta measure assists us to understand the volatility of each industry or firm by comparing it to the entire market. Hence, it reflects the risk (= volatility) of any firm compared to the entire market.

Here you may say: "What's in it for me? Why do I have to be bothered with this complicated stuff?"

I can understand you at this point, but I would like you to be aware that we are going to touch one of the most fascinating and important issues for you as a manager. We are going to disclose what is behind the **discount factor** that we use so extensively in **capital budgeting**. More than that, this factor enables you to distinguish between good and bad activity: what creates value, and what destroys value.

Measuring discount factor – in finance we used to say that for any risk, you require a better return. Why? You want to compensate yourself for the risk you took. The basic tool for that is the famous **CAPM (Capital Asset Pricing Model).** History note: Many scholars are responsible for this achievement. However, only Sharpe, Markowitz, and Merton Miller jointly received the 1990 Nobel Memorial Prize in Economics for this contribution. Back to work: the CAPM tries to predict (based on past events) the volatility (= risk) of the firm by comparing to the entire market. How does it work? The CAPM is trying to compensate in **two ways**:

(1) **Time value of money** ("the willingness to wait, to be patient"). **The time value of money** is represented by the **risk-free rate**. For a long-term investment, we usually use the example of a country of a ten-year government bond. This represents a risk-free rate, under the assumption that governments as a whole will stand behind their obligation. It is important to note that as the country becomes riskier, the yield will be higher: the wise investor will ask for higher compensation.

(2) **Risk**. Risk is represented by the beta (β) mentioned before. Take a look at Figure 4-5:

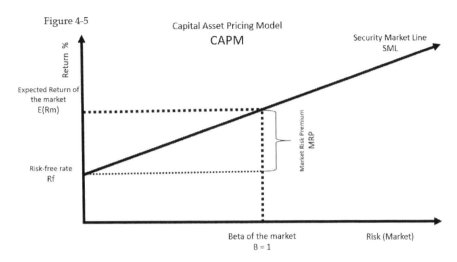

Figure 4-5

The basic formula:

$$\text{CAPM formula}$$
$$\text{Expected Return} = \text{Rf} + \beta \underbrace{\{E(Rm) - Rf\}}_{\substack{\text{Market Risk Premium} \\ \text{MRP}}}$$

Expected Return - the compensation for the risk of a specific investment.

Risk Free Rate (Rf) – when beta = 0. The number represents the yield of a ten-year government bond.

Expected return of the market - E(Rm). The compensation for the risk of the entire market.

Market Risk Premium (MRP) = The spread the market seeks as compensation for the risk between the risk-free rate and the expected return of the market.

Numeric example:

$$11 = 2 + 1.5\{8 - 2\}$$

Rf = 2
beta (β) = 1.5
E(Rm) = 8
Expected return = 11

Dear reader, the **expected return** is the MOST IMPORTANT number for you.

Note: For now, it will serve you as the **discount factor** for any capital budgeting project. In Chapter Six I will expand this model. It will serve as a hurdle rate to determine whether your project creates value or destroys value. It is the Required Rate of Return (RRR) to compensate the company for the risk it took while doing business. You will calculate it by comparing the hurdle rate with the return of doing business. So, let's take a look at the meaning of return.

Return is a profitability ratio that we take from the **economic domain:**

ROCE = NOPAT* / Economic Capital Employed**

As mentioned in the **Economic Domain**, the **ROCE** is THE **profitability ratio** that explains how many cents of profit (NOPAT) generates one dollar of **economic capital employed**. This ratio should be compared to **the hurdle rate**. Yes, we are now approaching the core of the Value Creation Concept: the return and risk relationship phenomenon.

Return and risk relationship. Or, how does the company create value?

After we struggled through too much technical stuff, we are well prepared for one simple argument:

When **ROCE > hurdle rate**, the company creates value. As simple as that.

When ROCE > hurdle rate, the company creates value

The company might have positive net profit, positive cash flow from operations, positive free cash flow, or any other measure or ratio you choose. It is all good and well, but the company **does not create value** on a sustainable basis unless it generates a better return at the hurdle rate. Why? As we learned before, the hurdle rate represents the risk that the company takes in order to create a sustainable competitive advantage. So, the **required rate of return** that the company needs is above the **hurdle rate**.

Let's go back to Part One. In Chapter One we elaborated on the meaning of **competitive advantage** from a few dimensions: economic, financial, technology, brand, and distribution channels. The **economic dimension** was all about **return**. The **financial dimension** was all about **risk**. We measured the **return** with the ROCE ratio. The **risk** we measured with the **hurdle rate**, the **Required Rate of Return**. The comparison between the two is illustrated in Figure 1-4 (which I borrowed from Chapter One).

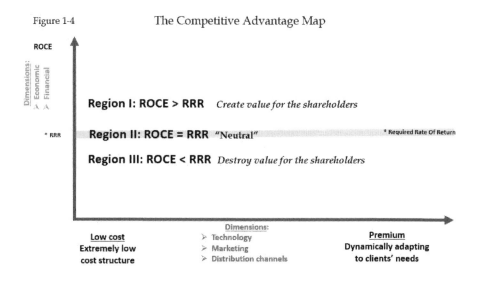

Figure 1-4   The Competitive Advantage Map

Figure 1-6 fused the ultimate intersection between strategy, economics and finance.

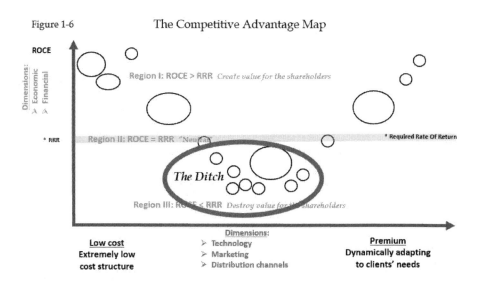

Figure 1-6   The Competitive Advantage Map

If the company wants to position itself at the competitive edge, it must generate return that is above the hurdle rate. If not, the company will find itself in The Ditch: it will not have the capabilities to allocate sufficient resources to create competitive advantage.

If the company wants to position itself at the competitive edge, it must generate return that is above the hurdle rate. If not, the company will find itself in The Ditch: it will not have the capabilities to allocate sufficient resources to create competitive advantage

---

The essence of this book is how to do it: how to develop **distinctive capabilities** in order to create a **competitive advantage** while keeping the Value Creation Concept in mind. This ensures that any project or activity nets you a return that is above the hurdle rate.

The essence of this book is how to do it: how to develop distinctive capabilities in order to create a competitive advantage

---

Lastly, I must confess, I did not tell you the whole story. Why? For the sake of the non-experts in accounting, economics, and finance. Now, we are at the stage where I can tell you that the **economic domain** and **the finance domain** live comfortably under the **corporate finance** umbrella. If you really want to sharpen your understanding about **corporate finance** and technical skills, please go to this website.[6] It will give you a wealth of knowledge, insights, and data. Enjoy.

---

[6] http://pages.stern.nyu.edu/~adamodar/New_Home_Page/home.htm

You just made a huge leap forward: this chapter is difficult to comprehend for non-experts in corporate finance. Chapter Five will give you managerial insights to boost your motivation to adopt the Value Creation Mindset. Chapter Six will equip you with the necessary tools to make it happen.

CHAPTER FIVE

MANAGERIAL IMPLICATIONS

Dear Reader,

If you feel you fully grasp the underlying concepts behind ensuring ROCE > RRR (Required Rate of Return), then you can omit this chapter.

But, if you would like to equip yourself with other managerial game plans, you may choose to keep on reading. It will be worthwhile. Promise.

Question: how would you rate your knowledge of corporate finance? If you feel you have a solid understanding of corporate finance, I warmly recommend you two sources:

1. A basic corporate finance book that is well studied in good MBA programs.[7]
2. A helpful website.[8]

Both will enrich your overall understanding and equip you with a wealth of up-to-date data.

If you feel this matter does not suit your curiosity, then you must make sure your CFO learns it by heart. This way you define the "**Why**" questions and the CFO furnishes the "**How**" and "**What**" questions.

Take note, this is the most important decision to make if you really want to grasp the **Value Creation Concept** that enables you to start your journey **From Enigma to Paradigm.**

---

[7] Example: Principles of Corporate Finance. Richard A. Brealey, Stewart C. Myers, Franklin Allen.

[8] Damodaran web site: http://pages.stern.nyu.edu/~adamodar/

If you choose to embark on your journey, then I want to believe that you agree with me that the following themes in corporate finance are extremely important for you:

1. NPV (Net Present Value)
2. CAPM (Capital Assets Pricing Model)
3. Real Option
4. Agency Theory

In the following pages and upcoming chapter, I will give life to these themes.

We already agree that your firm's ROCE in the long run should exceed the cost of capital. The conundrum is how to do it. Based on the discussion we held in Part One, we will to add to it the financial dimension.

In Part One we talked about two strategic phases:

1. GS – Growth Strategies
2. OS – Operation Strategies

GROWTH STRATEGIES (GS)

Growth Strategies deal with the unknown future: how to build appropriate **distinctive capabilities** to cope with opportunities and threats. In Part One we discuss few strategic methodologies to make it happen. Here, we will touch base with the financial dimensions to elucidate these strategic methodologies.

New strategic project:
Two types:

1. Tangible project
2. Intangible strategic project

* * *

1. Tangible project:

Warning: Management and directors LOVE tangible projects as they create optimism and growth attitudes. Beware, it's easy to convince them. Danger.

The basic theme of **the tangible project** is investing: making efforts that should bear fruit over multiple years.

Capital budgeting methodology deals with these **tangible investments**: new product lines, new technologies, new infrastructure, M&A, and the like. Capital budgeting takes care of these by utilizing the **NPV** (Net Present Value) practice. To start, prepare a multiannual cash flow for the entire project by completing these steps:

1. Define the investment (both capital expenditure and working capital).
2. Draw a picture of annual outcomes and inputs.
3. Bring yearly results to the initial meeting.
    a. The way to do this is by using the **DCF** (Discount Cash Flow) method.
    b. The discount factor is defined by the **CAPM** (Capital Assets Pricing Model). In essence, the discount factor reflects the risk of the project.
4. If the NPV > 0, that means that in the long run, if everything works as planned, ROCE > RRR. Hence, the project creates value for the shareholders.
    a. Why? Because the discount factor is the threshold: the minimum return you expect from the project.

Note: In Chapter Six we explore this in more practical detail. Here, I gave you just a taste.

* * *

Sometime your gut feeling tells you that a project is essential from a strategic standpoint. However, the NPV calculation appears to be negative. A popular countermeasure is to then "play" with the figures until the NPV become positive. Bad mistake. The NPV is your tool to examine your assumptions and forecasts. My advice is as follows: stick with your original NPV calculation and then thoroughly elaborate on your strategic assumptions.

If you still believe in the project, use the Real Option methodology, but only from a conceptual standpoint. Do not rush to work through the Real Option step by step. The core concept of Real Option is to increase the flexibility of decision-making processes later on.

The **Real Option** may be used when you feel you MUST prepare **distinctive capabilities** that cannot be justified by NPV calculation. After you use it to widen your options and prepare for the unknown future, ask your CFO to run through the appropriate mechanics of Real Option methodology.

To sum up, dealing with the future is a risky business. Remember that in corporate finance, risk is not "good" or "bad." Risk is the way to quantify the volatilities from the past and reflect it into the unknown future. The following tools give you some comfort to make such calculated decisions: NPV, CAPM, DCF and Real Option.

2. Intangible strategic project:

Warning: Management and directors DO NOT like intangible projects. It creates a feeling of: "Well, we don't know…we cannot justify it with data and rational thinking…we do not understand it." These are the type of arguments (and much harsher) you will hear.

But, I would urge you to reconsider. This is exactly how to acquire **distinctive capabilities** that will be at the forefront of coping with an unknown future. This is exactly the conundrum you are facing along your journey From Enigma to Paradigm. This is the heart of the Value Creation Concept. Hint: What is the definition of **luck** in **business**? **"When opportunity meets capability."**

Luck? When opportunity meets capability

The word **"intangible"** implies that an ordinary businessperson cannot get it. Only a businessperson well-equipped with both broad and in-depth knowledge of the company's business cluster can appreciate the relevance of developing new, **distinctive capabilities**.

In Chapter One we elaborated how to estimate your **competitive advantage** through **strategic lenses**: technology, brand recognition, and distribution channels. Then, we added the economic and financial dimensions. The differentiation analyses and development you complete in order to gain the competitive advantage involves a deep understanding of the ecosystem you work within. See Figure 2-3 for an illustration. You must build **distinctive capabilities** required by the business partners within your ecosystem.

You must build distinctive capabilities required by the business partners within your ecosystem

---

Figure 2-3

The Ecosystem Approach

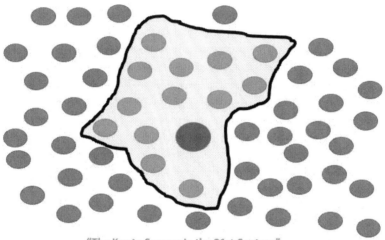

"The Key to Success in the 21st Century"

If you want to be recognized as a **critical partner** by your ecosystem, you must develop **unique intangible assets** that contribute to your cluster.

Sorry, this does not come without the risk of developing intangibles that are not going to generate cash. You can think about this process in terms of Real Option: onboard capabilities that enlarge the decision-making flexibility for the future.

Companies that do not create **distinctive capabilities** for coping in the future either do not have the will, intellectual capabilities, or are simply are low on cash. Companies like this fall into The Ditch, as illustrated in Figure 1-6.

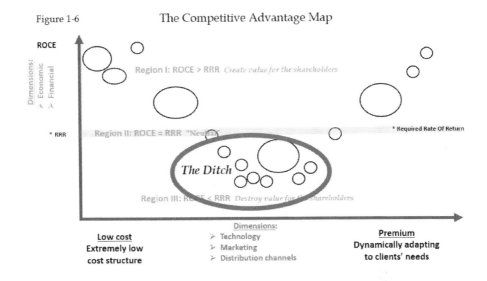

Figure 1-6   The Competitive Advantage Map

These companies end up with economic performance best described as ROCE (Return on Capital Employed) less than RRR (Required Rate of Return):

ROCE < RRR

Hence, their value is destroyed for their shareholders.

From my humble observation, the remedy for this is to invest heavily and wisely in **intangibles**. Yes, easy to ignore and easy to blame as unnecessary or even wasteful *in the moment*. However, I think that these are the secret weapons that create value on a sustainable and long-term basis.

In Chapter Six, I will outline how to invest in intangible strategic projects in a way that's easier to swallow by the ordinary businessperson.

Remember, the tension between the short-termism and long-termism approaches are at the heart of the Value Creation Concept.

Remember, the tension between the short-termism and long-termism approaches are at the heart of the Value Creation Concept

---

OPERATION STRATEGIES (OS)

Operation Strategies deal with the following phenomena: how to generate more and more cash from the current capabilities that the company owns:

1. Capital employed
2. Human capital, and
3. Social capital

Part three is fully dedicated to elaborating the strategies and managerial methodologies of building and harvesting **human** and **social capital**. This is the most dramatic contribution to the Value Creation Concept: the **human factor**. The business sphere pays lip service to the **human factor** with all kinds of mumbo jumbo language that can be summarized in a few words: the working environment should be characterized by **mutual trust** and **respect** among the entire business sphere. Easier said than done. Harvesting the capital employed belongs to this chapter. The question is how to build a **measurement system** that will **align** the **interests** of the **entire workforce**. How to squeeze a few more drops from the lemon, again and again.

Let's return to the basics:

The overall aim of the company is ROCE > Cost of Capital. Please note that RRR (Required Rate of Return) is equal to the Cost of Capital.

This is the way a company creates value: the **Return on Capital Employed** is greater than the **risk** of **making business** within a **specific industry**.

Hence, our aim is to increase the **ROCE** above the **Required Rate of Return**.

Let's take a look at the components of ROCE.

We start with the simple equation:

$$\text{ROCE} = \text{Operation Profit} / \text{Capital Employed}$$

With algebra, we can expand it to the following components (notice that "Sales" on both sides can be eliminated, hence, the equation remains the same):

$$\text{Operation Profit} / \text{Sales} \quad \mathbf{X} \quad \text{Sales} / \text{Capital Employed}$$

Now, let's dive into the basic components. We call them **"Value Drivers."**

Figure 5-1 provides an introductory illustration of how to break down the ROCE into meaningful value drivers. You might want to personalize it to your particular firm.

The "secret" here is to aim for the overall measure (ROCE), and to give the right measure for each team within the company. The right measure should reflect the line of sight and influence of each working team. This is the basis of the measuring system that will support decisionmakers to utilize and monetize the current capital employed in its best form.

Figure 5-1

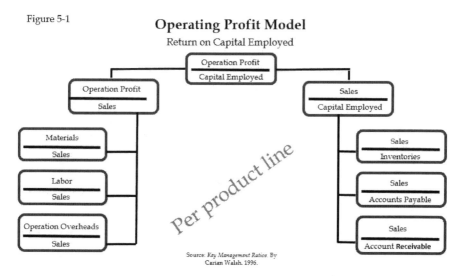

Operating Profit Model

Return on Capital Employed

Source: *Key Management Ratios.* By Carian Walsh. 1996.

In summary:

Growth Strategies prepare the company for the unknown future. There are two types of initiatives:

1. **Tangible projects**

   Invest in new projects that can be "touched" such as infrastructure, machinery, and the like. These projects are measured by NPV (Net Present Value). If the NPV > 0, the project should be accepted since the planned ROCE > cost of capital. If the NPV < 0, the project should not be accepted unless it creates flexibility that's worth the effort. Unfortunately, the math behind the NPV calculation looks like rocket science to the ordinary businessperson, and hence they love it. Without too many questions, I might add. Sad. Good businesspeople should cope with the assumptions and the strategy behind it.

2. **Intangible strategic projects**
   Investing in new projects that cannot be "touched."
   Intangible strategic projects mostly deal with preparing the
   company for the unknown future by developing **distinctive
   capabilities**. These enable the company to position itself as
   the **desired business partner** within its **ecosystem**. Again,
   here the wise businessperson uses the Real Option concept
   to make his/her own judgement call to justify the particular
   intangible strategic project.

Proponents of corporate finance claim that it addresses the
unknown future with ammunition, not just math. It also addresses
the **behavior aspect: agency theory**. One might argue that **agency
theory** falls under managerial aspects. This is true, but since it was
pioneered within the corporate finance sphere, I will expand on it
briefly.

Agency theory deals with **human behavioral phenomena,**
specifically, human behavior that detracts from doing effective
business.

**Agency theory deals with human behavioral phenomena,
specifically, human behavior that detracts from doing effective
business.**

Agency theory[9] deals with conflicts of interest that lie deep within
corporate culture. Specifically, the disparate attitudes between the

---

[9] Jensen, Michael C. and William H. Meckling. 1976. Theory of the firm: Managerial
behavior, agency costs and ownership structure. Journal of Financial Economics (October),
3(4): 305–360. https://www.sfu.ca/~wainwrig/Econ400/jensen-meckling.pdf

principal, the company owner, and the agent who is supposed to create value for the principal. This is just a rough outline, but you can apply it to all corporate components. Each working team and individual has another set of interests within the company. The remedies for this are of two types:

1. **Corporate governance principles**: rules, performance measurement, remuneration policy, and the like. Corporate governance can be observed as a somewhat **exogenous tool**. Trying to align dissimilar interests with **rules** and **procedures**.

2. **Management**. The managerial mindset that we will cover in Part Three remedies from a more **internal standpoint**: how to **stir the behavior of the entire workforce from within.**

In this chapter, I gave you a few managerial tools that enable you to harvest the basic themes of corporate finance to your advantage. In Chapter Six we add more tools that sharpen your corporate finance knowledge to your needs.

CHAPTER SIX

TOOLS & PRACTICES

In this chapter, I present the mechanics of the ideas described in the last two chapters: the how to.

Basically, there are two extreme ways to deal with these concepts:

1. The "right" way: thoroughly and with all the nitty-gritty details that consultants love. This will cost you trouble and money. Sometimes, going this way will look like an asymptote in math: coming closer and closer to the end results, but never reaching it.
2. The "wrong" way: some consultants call it "quick and dirty," or "let's make it happen NOW."

As you become familiar with my style, you may have guessed that I prefer the second way. Correct. The reason for this is simple, I advocate the affect that it has at the cost of accuracy. Life, and managerial life in particular, are all about making it happen. So, let's take the "wrong" way.

THE MIGRATION FROM ACCOUNTING TO ECONOMICS

Migrating from accounting to economics requires a change in mindset and basic methodologies. In this chapter, you will discover the basic mechanics of this essential transformation. At the core of the migration are two interrelated statements that influence each other:

1. Economic Balance Sheet statement
2. Economic P&L (Profit and Loss) statement

* * *

ECONOMIC BALANCE SHEET STATEMENT

As we summed up in Chapter Four, the **accountants'** view is that the company's **capital employed** consists of fixed assets (**without the intangible**) plus working capital (**current assets minus the entire current liabilities**).

The **economists'** view is that the company's capital employed consists of fixed assets (**including the intangible**), plus working capital (**current assets minus non-interest-bearing current liability**). This measurement system encourages managers to make wise decisions by taking a long-term view.

Here you can see it in two charts:

Figure 4-3

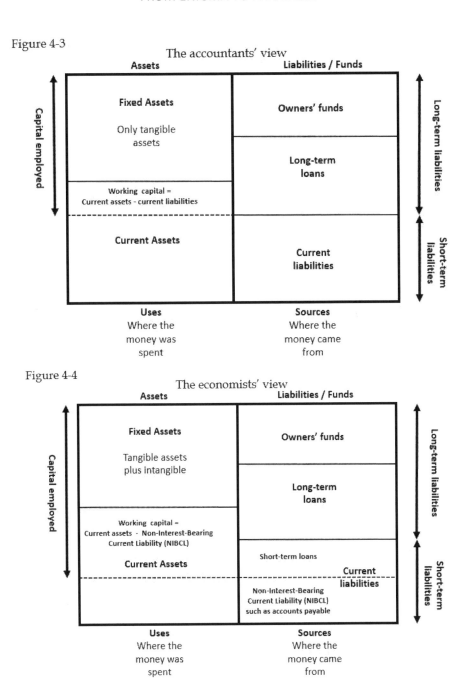

Figure 4-4

In the next section, you will find guiding principles on how to incorporate the **intangible** and **strategic investments** within the economic balance sheet statement.

GUIDING PRINCIPLES FOR CAPITALIZING INTANGIBLES

Assume that you are facing an R&D project. The related equipment and other infrastructure you purchased are not costs, since the matching principle guides you to code these as fixed assets. Later on, you deduct the value from these related fixed assets on an annual basis (depreciation). This deduction will appear on the P&L (Profit & Loss) statement as annual depreciation. Simple.

Now, what about other expenses like hiring engineers, materials consumed, research services purchased, travel, professional consulting, and the like? Accounting principles push these to the P&L statement. Poor choice. The migration to the economic sphere requires coding them exactly like equipment purchased. Code them as fixed assets. The trick here is simple:

First, identify the R&D project as a "closed" project that requires a comprehensive business plan.

Second, all the efforts and costs should be capitalized and placed under the name of the project in the economic balance sheet. Continue to do so until the project begins generating cash flow.

Third, decide the economic lifetime of the project. For the sake of simplicity, let's say it's five years.

Fourth, after the project starts to generate cash flow, deduct 20% on an annual basis, assuming that the economic life of the project is five years.

Figure 6-1 give you a nice illustration:

Figure 6-1

R&D Project #1

Investment in:
Fixed Assets: equipment, buildings
Salaries for engineers and experts
Materials consumed
Research that was purchased
Travels
Professional fees: experts, consultants

Total

Fruitful economic life of the project

Depreciation rate

As simple as that. Omit the calls to make it much more accurate. Instead, make it simple.

These guiding principles pair nicely with many other intangibles. You may want to adjust here and there, but basically, these guiding principles lead managers to invest in the future of the company because it doesn't ruin the bottom line of the economic P&L statement.

This way, we resolve the ongoing conflict between the strategy and the quarterly and annual performance of your company. The Board will like it, the financial analysts will appreciate it, and the Market will behave accordingly.

STRATEGIC INVESTMENT

Strategic investment is an investment you cannot justify with regular capital budgeting tools like NPV. Basically, it becomes a dead end project. Sometimes, managers believe this kind of investment is essential because it will create more opportunities, and hence flexibilities, for future decision-making. This we call **strategic investment**.

Strategic investment is an investment you cannot justify with regular capital budgeting tools like NPV

The mechanical way to deal with strategic investment is pretty similar to capitalized intangibles. In both cases, during the period of **building distinctive capabilities**, you code them as fixed assets under the project name. Once the strategic investment starts to generate cash, you depreciate it according to the economic life of the strategic investment.

Comments:
These two examples shed light on a few phenomena:
1. The **investment period**, characterized by gathering the entirety of expenses into one body of the project.
2. The **utilization period**, characterized by depreciation that considers the economic life of the project.

3. As long as the project hasn't started to generate cash, it's included in the **economic capital employed**. Therefore, it will only carry capital costs, as I'll describe later when we deal with the economic P&L statement.
4. If the project will not generate cash in the feasible future, the entire project should be a write-off; it should be eliminated from the economic balance sheet at once and recorded as one-off cost in the P&L statement.

Here is the most important lesson to draw your attention to:

What is the essence of **capital employed**?

Answer: The amount of money, "capital," that management uses while generating business.

Capital employed: the amount of money the management uses while generation business

---

Remember: using capital employed costs money. It does not matter how the company finances it. Hence, it is part of generating business that the management pays for.

As the management reduces the amount of capital employed, it will reduce the cost of generating business. This way, management will not only look at expenses how accountants look at them, but instead will consider the entire cost of generating business.

This way, management will not only look at expenses how accountants look at them, but instead will consider the entire cost of generating business

---

In the next section, you will find the basic calculation for the use of capital, a.k.a. the **capital charge**.

ECONOMIC PROFIT & LOSS STATEMENT

The most important distinction between the way accountants view P&L statements and the way economists see them is as follows:
A. Expenses that have impact on the long-term state of the company. We called them **intangibles**. I think that we took a sufficient amount of time to explain them intuitively, as well as how to deal with them, in the previous pages.
B. The cost of generating business from the capital employed perspective, the **capital charge**. Now, I assume you are familiar with the reasoning behind it. So, let's get to the mechanics.

Capital charge is the amount of **capital employed** multiplied by the **cost of capital**.

Capital charge is the amount of capital employed multiplied by the cost of capital

---

In Chapter Four, we invested a sufficient amount of time to understand the **cost of capital** phenomena from the shareholders' perspective.
Cost of capital = Required Rate of Return (RRR). In essence, it is the **Required Rate of Return** that compensates the company on the risk it took while doing business.

In essence, it is the Required Rate of Return that compensates the company on the risk it took while doing business

---

When we dealt with capital employed, I told you that you should not consider how you finance it. However, when computing the RRR, we have to consider how the company finances its operations. The technical term in finance for "cost of capital" is WACC (Weighted Average Cost of Capital).

I'll explain it in brief:

All sources of capital are included in the WACC.

To calculate WACC, multiply the cost of each capital component by its proportional weight, and take the sum of the results. The method for calculating WACC can be expressed in the following formula:

WACC formula

$$WACC = \frac{E}{V} \times Re + \frac{D}{V} \times Rd \times (1 - Tc)$$

Components:

Re = Cost of equity

Rd = Cost of debt

E = Market value of the firm's equity

D = Market value of the firm's debt

V = E + D = Total market value of the firm's financing (equity and debt)

E/V = Percentage of the financing that is equity

D/V = Percentage of the financing that is debt

Tc = Corporate tax rate

Re = Cost of equity. We covered the cost of equity when we reviewed the CAPM model. This is the minimal RRR (Required Rate of Return) that the shareholder seeks for the risk they take when giving their money to the company.

Rd = Cost of debt. This is the cost to use the money you borrowed from debt providers (such as banks and others). Since interest expense is an expense, there is a tax shield. A **tax shield** is a reduction in the taxes that the government takes from your company. It is a way to save cash. Meaning that the government takes part of this particular expense, known as interest expense. This is why the after-tax cost of debt is Rd (1 – corporate tax rate). Broadly speaking, there are two types of capital providers:

I.   Equity - shareholders' money, and

II.   Debt - lenders that require the money back at an agreed time, plus interest for the use of the money.

WACC is the average of the costs of these sources of money, each weighted by its proportional usage.

When we've covered the RRR (Required Rate of Return), we have only done so from a narrow scope: the shareholders'. Now is the time to widen our scope to include the debt providers. Hence, WACC can be perceived as the **overall Required Rate of Return** to the **stakeholders** that equips the firm with capital (money) for shareholders and debt providers.

Now, we are ready to better understand the meaning and the mechanics of capital charge.

Capital charge is the amount of **capital employed** multiplied by the **cost of capital**.

Capital employed we reviewed at the beginning of this chapter.

Cost of capital we just discussed a couple pages ago.

Coming back to the **Economic Profit & Loss statement**, the bottom line of the statement is the EVA[10] (Economic Value Added). There are several names for it, but the rationale and the techniques are pretty much the same. Some examples are Economic Profit (EP), Value Based Management (VBM), and others.

The basic formula:
+ Accountant's Operation Profit (what you can find in the regular P&L)
- Intangibles (as described in Figure 6-1)
+ Tax (add the tax)
= NOPAT (Net Operation Profit After Tax)
- Capital Charge
= EVA (Economic Value Added)

In this chapter, I presented you with the essential tools and practices to overcome the conceptual gap when you explore the **Value Creation Concept**. This is vital if you want to embark on your journey **From Enigma to Paradigm**.
In the next part of the book, Part Three, we will explore how to tie everything together; how to make it happen from the managerial standpoint.

Important note: I elaborated on the mechanics and techniques of the **Economic Balance sheet statement** and the **Economic Profit & Loss statement** in a way to ignite your thinking. If you would like more comprehensive materials, I urge you to look at Professor

---

[10] In my mind, that is the most important application (usage) of corporate finance theories of the last 50 years. Pioneered by Joel Stern. The consultancy firm, Stern Stewart & Co. made it a popular element of configuring a performance measurement system.

Damodaran's website [11]. Professor Damodaran will equip you with extensive supplementary materials including tables, data, explanation, and practical tools.

---

[11] http://pages.stern.nyu.edu/~adamodar/

PART THREE:

MANAGEMENT,

THE VALUE CREATION

MINDSET

CHAPTER SEVEN

INTUITION, FUNDAMENTALS

AND PRINCIPLES

"Nowadays people know the price of everything and the value of nothing." (Oscar Wilde)

"Know much, understand little."
One might know a lot.
The problem is how much one understands.
The barrier is how much one can implement their understanding.
This is the human challenge; in this respect, the managerial arena
is only the micro cosmos of humankind.

Value creation, what a fascinating term. Since the dawn of humankind, our focus has been how to improve our lives. In the early beginning, it was all about feeding the family that day.

Later, when people started to develop and learn about agriculture, it lengthened the time horizon: one planted a seed, and yielded dozens of crops, short-term. One planted a tree and got thousands of fruits that lasted for a much longer period of time. One hunted an animal and had meat for a short time. One raised an animal, and got many different types of nourishment which lasted a long while: eggs, milk, meat, and leather. Note: Short-termism and long-termism were at war from the earliest era. It was defined by the activities of individuals, families, and small communities. When people discovered strength in numbers, small communities became larger organizations.

In both families and small communities, **sense of ownership** was the strongest driver of value creation.

In both families and small communities, sense of ownership was the strongest driver of value creation.

Activities were aimed to improve the life of the individual and their immediate family. In larger organizations, the alignment of interests started to break. In finance we call it the agency phenomenon: the interests of the stakeholders depart from each other. When this happens, **value creation** is not the highest priority of the entire community of stakeholders.

Part Three tries to solve this misalignment. We claim that the secret is all about sense of ownership. How to develop and maintain a **sense of ownership** is the core of Part Three.

Our aim is to explore it in a way that ignites further ideas in you, dear reader.

I was born and raised in a small community called a kibbutz. It was operated under pure Communist ideology: you contribute as much as you can, and get only what you need. There was no connection between your salary and your contribution.

During my 20s, I worked in a small farm that belonged to the kibbutz. It was meaningful for both myself and the rest of the workers. We ploughed, planted, cultivated, irrigated and harvested. We showed our influence. We worked in a small team with a huge amount of motivation. We wanted to create value.

Value, at that time, was to increase the crops as much as possible, per acre and per cubic meter of water.

Every evening we sat together in the dining hall and planned the next day. We felt like a family. We did not pay attention to hours of work or efforts. All we wanted to do was improve. We felt a great deal of **ownership**: it was "our" farm. We did not expect any materialistic gain. We lived in a very modest environment.

Later on, I moved to an industrial environment where the politics around me was much more obvious. Although, it was the same kind of community, a kibbutz, many more people were influenced by the divisions of labor: each had done the same activities for years. People were measured by the numbers of units they passed through the process. As a result, they could not connect their efforts with the overall outcome. Though again, there was no connection between efforts and personal gain, one could feel that the sense of ownership was much weaker.

This was my early personal experience dealing with value creation. Now, for more than 25 years, I have been exploring the **Value Creation Phenomenon**. I have done it from different angles: as a CFO, Human Resources Director, and consultant. I strongly believe in the connection between **value creation** and **sense of ownership**. I think it is the key to improve the level of value creation in any organization.

If you ask an executive about **sense of ownership**, you will be surprised at how supportive they are. No question about it. However, here is the minefield: it looks different across various levels of the organization. Executives cannot understand this. They have forgotten the early days when they served downstairs.

Worse, when executives talk about **sense of ownership**, their team develops a great deal of cynicism and skepticism. I believe that this is a dangerous issue, as it does not create the atmosphere for **value creation**. In economics we say that it **destroys value**.

Why is it that in small groups we feel differently? Why, in a small team, do people tend to feel more entrepreneurial? What is lost when an organization grows?

Think about a start-up: the level of passion and innovation. What is the reason for the dramatic change in behavior when these people arrive at a larger organization?

What do we miss in our understanding? How we can manage things differently?

Let's explore it.

VALUE CREATION IS THE ESSENCE OF HUMANKIND

We sense joy and happiness whenever we feel that we created value. This is the center of human behavior. Accomplish a goal, then feel that others need us, or admire our contribution. Why does the managerial arena neglect this? Managers do say it is important, but when they need to pay for it with their behavior or currency, it doesn't happen.

Value creation is the essence of humankind

I think that the reason is that management as a profession has not progressed for decades. Moses was the first person to start the managerial profession by establishing a clear definition of governing people. In the late 19th century, few thinkers took the managerial profession forward. The emergence of the big conglomerate in the early 20th century forced managers to harvest the latest theories: **division of labor, command and control,** and **measurement systems** that highlighted **efficiency** over **effectiveness**. The basic assumption was that a few people knew better than others, and they would create an atmosphere for everyone. Some even rushed to the wording of "**scientific management**." Their claim was that management was a science that brings results, not a social activity.

Division of labor, command and control, and measurement systems that highlighted efficiency over effectiveness

---

To give some justification to "**scientific management**," we could say that the mass production era required this management style. But the quality of life of the people within those big conglomerates was miserable. They were bored and frustrated. Yes, quality of life from a materialistic standpoint increased dramatically during this era, just not for the people who went to work and wasted time until they returned home. They were tired and bored. [Side note: Perhaps a few of the social ills that came to light later on, such as alcoholism and domestic violence, were encouraged by this sort of work environment]. The senior people tried their best to create value. However, the rank and file was unimpressed. They were told what to do, and were supposed to do it. Period.

In management literature, this is called **Management 1.0**. One could claim it was good enough for the industrial environment, but is not suitable for our current era.

In 1999, Peter F. Drucker described the weaknesses of **Management 1.0** at length in his book *Management Challenges for the 21st Century*. He elaborated on the challenges for different management practices and the measurement system to judge them, but he was too late to lay the groundwork for **Management 2.0**.

In 2007, Gary Hamel took it on himself to facilitate a new agenda for management strategy in his book *The Future of Management*. Later on, he established The MIX (Management Innovation eXchange) website to encourage scholars and practitioners to develop **Management 2.0**.

MANAGEMENT 1.0

The official father of **Management 1.0** is Frederick W. Taylor. He was the pioneer of the "**scientific management**" movement, named so because management is science, he claimed. The essence of Management 1.0 is: only a few can understand it, and they will instruct the others. That may sound weird, but current management practices have not changed much.

Frederick W. Taylor's approach was very basic: the common person has no brain. He owns two hands and we are going to hire only his hands. Period.

Scientific management diagnosed the mission of production, and cut it into very small tasks that were easy to perform and easy to teach. The slogan was **efficiency** and the tools were stopwatches and other means of control. It was termed "division of labor." The ideology was pretty simple: manpower is cheap and should be easy to replace. The large conglomerates then started to produce cars, machinery, and engage in other heavy manufacturing processes.

Scientific management diagnosed the mission of production, and cut it into very small tasks that were easy to perform and easy to teach. The slogan was efficiency and the tools were stopwatches and other means of control. It was termed "division of labor."

In the thick of Management 1.0 and the Industrial Revolution, the workforce was ideal for scientific management practices. It also nicely suited the poor people who migrated from foreign countries or from rural areas to the cities. Why? These people had just left poverty for the lower middle class. They needed constant levels of income, no matter what. They leased their two hands, built a nice family, and hoped that the next generation would have better education and, ultimately, better jobs. The industry itself was not under pressure from real competitive forces.

Because the focus was on **division of work** and **efficiency**, the effort was to reduce the level of input (materials and working hours) to the bare minimum. The entire management regime could be summed up in two words: **command and control**. It was the best means for the mass production era, of which the Black Ford

Model T was the defining symbol. The ideology was to bring consumer goods to a much wider audience. The level of income was supposed to be sufficient to consume the goods the firms produced using the best practices of scientific management.

Because the focus was on division of work and efficiency, the effort was to reduce the level of input (materials and working hours) to the bare minimum. The entire management regime could be summed up in two words: command and control

---

Global forces migrated these managerial practices to developing countries. The low wages in these developing countries started to bring another level of competition to international firms. As scientific management became common practice in the mass manufacturing arena, many scholars started to dislike its meaning and connotation, so they tried to cover it with much nicer envelopes and wording. They thought it was not human enough, and was not the right way to motivate people. However, if one peels a few layers from the onion, one finds the solid core of the **scientific management, Management 1.0.**

There is no argument that Management 1.0 was very important for the entire 20th century. It was the right practice for the society of that time, both the industry and the people. Cheap goods, and a steady stream of income for the emerging middle class.

In summary, there is a new quality of life for many hundreds of millions of people worldwide. Even today, this is the major motivation to pull another few hundreds of millions of people from poverty in the East: China, India, Vietnam, Bangladesh, Thailand, and other tigers.

If we want to sum it up: cheap labor, cheap products, and a low level of constant income fuel each other under the regime of Management 1.0.

MANAGEMENT 2.0

Peter F. Drucker is the godfather of Management 2.0. In 1999, he published *Management Challenges for the 21st Century*. There, he underlines many issues and themes that would dictate the bedrock of new management practices. He debates issues like: **new paradigms in management, knowledge workers, challenges from measurement systems**, and more. Around the year Drucker published his book, the new economy emerged. The economy that put **knowledge** at its center.

The new economy put knowledge at its center

The bust of the dotcom economy in the early 21st century only increased the pace of the new economy. The overcapacity of infrastructure sped up the pace of the new economy. Many manufacturing industries migrated to the Far East, and new industries emerged in the West. Most of these new industries in the West required another style of management. The second and third generation of immigrants were not prepared to use their hands and leave their brains at the gate. They looked for another kind of occupation, a meaningful work.

The second and third generation of immigrants were not prepared to use their hands and leave their brains at the gate. They looked for another kind of occupation, a meaningful work

---

These two tectonic shifts are pivotal in order to understand the Management 2.0 era.

THE NEW INDUSTRIES

Looking into the S&P 500 by decade from the mid-20th century until present day, one can gain very valuable insights. Somewhere around the late eighties, the landscape was starting to change. Firms that were completely new jumped at the first raw opportunity. They came from nowhere. Most of them were pioneered in the garage of their founders. They suggested to the world new kinds of services that nobody even dreamed of before. These services were rendered in completely new technologies.

The pace of the emergence of these new companies was coupled with the disappearance of many firms. All of a sudden, the economy become very fragile. A company could emerge and gain huge success, then after several years, disappear. Either by M&A, or when new technologies disrupt the older company's business model. One of the most influential economists during the 20th century was **Joseph Schumpeter** (1883-1950). Mr. Schumpeter was the first to identify this **creative destruction**: new technologies that destroy old technologies.

At that point, many scholars and practitioners started to challenge the old style of managing. The new firms asked for well-educated and highly motivated employees. The firms badly needed both the **brain and** the **heart** of their employees. Leave the brain at the gate? Are you kidding? These new companies gained their **competitive edge** by having the best talents.

The new firms asked for well-educated and highly motivated employees. The firms badly needed both the brain and the heart of their employees. Leave the brain at the gate? Are you kidding?

The "problem" with talented people is that they do not like to be managed at all; especially not under the old style of **command and control**. It is quite a phenomenon to see that the best new companies are think tanks of sorts with non-management leaders. Leaders that did not study management, leaders with no past experience in the old regime of management practices.

It is quite a phenomenon to see that the best new companies are think tanks of sorts with non-management leaders. Leaders that did not study management, leaders with no past experience in the old regime of management practices.

The founders lead and manage their firms with their unique style. No one can say whether it is good or bad. It is a fact. In management literature, many books tried to make the case for success and failure stories. The authors tried to make generalizations and build new theories of Dos and Don'ts in management. This wealth of ideas was good. Good in the sense that it gave a wake-up call to managers and leaders. Curious managers found themselves in havoc: too many contradictory theories and methodologies.

In parallel emerged yet another school of thought: the **human behavior** and **organizational scholars**. They tried to fix the managerial landscape by patching in their new theories. Their intention was good, to put the human being at the center of management; the needs of the human being as the driving force of motivation. The problem with this school of thought is that there is no holistic approach to managing a firm.

Motivational theories are crucial for managing people. However, one should have a holistic understanding of other forces: technology, geopolitics, demographic, economics, behavioral economics, finance, operations, and marketing, and then wrap it all up in a decent managerial framework.

It is obvious that these new industries desired a new way of managing. Furthermore, the conventional industries had changed: they could no longer claim that their employees need to leave their brains at the gate. The intense competition from the global economy requires a new type of employee, an employee using their **brain** and their **heart**.

Again, the motivation narrative from human behavior experts looks today like aspirin for cancer: it might reduce the pain for a short period, it might treat the symptom, but cannot heal the source of the problem.

We need **Management 2.0**, and thanks to Peter F. Drucker, we have a few milestones to start our journey.

THE SECOND AND THIRD GENERATION OF IMMIGRANTS

As we mentioned, the needs of the first generation of immigrants were pretty simple: shelter, nutrition, and a constant stream of income. These were their wishes. But their main goal was the best education they could get for the second generation. They wanted to secure for their kids the best future possible.

The needs of the first generation of immigrants were pretty simple: shelter, nutrition, and a constant stream of income

---

These first generation immigrants saved penny to penny to ensure they would have enough wealth to give their kids the best education. Their kids studied, and were well equipped to argue against the "hands for hire" ethos developed by **Frederick Taylor**. These kids grew up and developed their own tastes: they had options. They could decide where and how to work. Not only were employers choosing their employees, but employees decided which kind of employer they would like to have.

What are the new criteria for the working environment? The main one is **meaningful work**. We spend one third of our life in the workplace. We want a place that will fulfill our wishes, our dreams. We want to influence the future of the firm, as well as our own future.

What are the new criteria for the working environment? The main one is meaningful work. We want a place that will fulfill our wishes, our dreams. We want to influence the future of the firm, as well as our own future.

This kind of working environment needs another kind of management regime. But well-founded management practices are not yet fully baked. The nice band-aids that were adopted by many are a good starting point.

The firms that emerged from the garages of entrepreneurs were better equipped for this new type of employee. The founders of these firms knew what they did not like, and they tried their best to make the managerial environment more flat and democratic with fewer layers of managers. They tried to build the **informal relationships** that would overcome the formal **organizational chart**.

The new entrepreneurs tried to build the informal relationships that would overcome the formal organizational chart

---

When these companies were small enough, it worked great. The coffee machine was the best place to exchange views and make decisions. Formal decision processes were looked at as rather weird and old fashioned. This entrepreneurship environment was like the new kid on the block. Business literature exploded with success stories. However, too many scholars looked at these success stories and tried to make generalizations, to build a theory as a form of reverse engineering. If it works at great companies like *XYZ*, they concluded, then it is *the* new management methodology.

However, this is not the way to build a theory. Good theory cannot be grounded on examples, as Management 1.0 proved: a successful theory must act like a framework that serves many landscapes and circumstances. Even today, Management 1.0 serves manufacturing, governments, NGOs, and not-for-profit organizations very well. Each sector adopts it differently. But the basic characteristics remain the same: a **command & control environment**, a focus on **efficiency**, and **division of labor**. To sum it up, the many that **do not know**, and the few that **do know**.

This managerial framework served the needs of the economy, and society at large during the 20th century. The current economy and society do not need the Management 1.0 regime, even with newer motivational psychology band-aids. Our era deserves revolution, a new framework: Management 2.0.

Before we continue our journey, we have to examine another phenomenon: those that claim they are operating in the new managerial landscape. We would like very much to agree with them, but we must draw a fine line between Management 1.0 and Management 2.0. This distinction is necessary. Why? We do not claim that Management 1.0 has no role any more. On the contrary. There are business environments that certainly need the characteristics of Management 1.0. However, it is crucial that business people understand what kind of management style their business requires.

It is crucial that business people understand what kind of management style their business requires

---

Now we have arrived, and are well prepared for the aim of this book:

How can we assist **manufacturing SMEs** (Small Medium Enterprises)? This is the core of our journey **From Enigma to Paradigm.**

How can we assist manufacturing SMEs ? This the core of our journey From Enigma to Paradigm.

Unfortunately, manufacturing SMEs were not part of the progress that benefitted the High Tech industry.
Therefore, this book is **dedicated** to **SME manufacturing companies**. I truly believe that these companies have been steered by the wrong strategic and managerial methodologies. It is quite different to follow an adult elephant, to understand his daily routine, than to figure out how he became so big and mature.

It is quite different to follow an adult elephant, to understand his daily routine, than to figure out how he became so big and mature.

Strategic literature offers "love stories" about the hero that made it, propagating an archetype that does not suit manufacturing SMEs. Therefore, this book **focuses** on **strategic matters**, and the **support tools** required, from two disciplines: **Corporate Finance** and **Management**.

The previous Part, Part Two, dealt with **Corporate Finance**. This Part will explore a few managerial dimensions that make the successful strategy a reality.

The next book in this series will dive much deeper into the managerial dimension. Here, we only give you a direction for the mindset, and a few handy tools. Stay tuned.

As mentioned before, the **core** of this book is how to make the **entire cluster** into **collaborators: participants that are dynamically looking to satisfy the end users.** This cannot be done with a few geniuses that know everything. It involves making each firm a lab for **creativity: products, technologies, services,** and **practices.** In order to do this, each workforce member must feel a **sense of ownership**.

Nowadays, it is common to talk about the efficiency gap: that the improvement in productivity rate is declining. Most management literature is thinly veiled complaints about the willingness to invest.

This book argues that the efficiency gap can be treated from a completely different angle: how to improve in **productivity** from the **managerial aspect**.

This insight is the core of this book.

In the next chapter, we deal with managerial implications: what takeaways you can gain from the Value Creation Mindset.

This book argues that the efficiency gap can be treated from a completely different angle: how to improve in productivity from the managerial aspect.

CHAPTER EIGHT

MANAGERIAL IMPLICATIONS

Introduction:
Our prime audience, SME manufacturing managers, lead us to unique frameworks that nicely suit the SME manufacturing segment's needs. However, here is an overview of the three parts of this book that apply to all managers.

OVERVIEW OF THE BOOK

1. **Part One** focused on revolutionary concepts that create a **competitive advantage** in three dimensions: technology, economics, and finance. This should create the edge to be a **respected business partner** within your **ideal cluster**.
2. **Part Two** explored the **Value Creation Concept** in its more technical aspects: accounting, economics, and financials.
    a. **Accounting** provides history in a robust manner.
    b. **Economics** translates the accounting into the manager's language: what are the data and the platforms needed to make decisions?
    c. **Financial**s bring the future: how to deal with risk by making decisions that ultimately relate to the unknown future.
3. **Part Three** encapsulates the first two Parts into a managerial framework: how it should be done, and the roadmap to make it happen.

Chapter Seven explored the Value **Creation Mindset** from three standpoints: history, socioeconomics, and managerial developments.

In this chapter, we will discuss the managerial implications:

1. What outcomes should firms should expect to gain?
2. And hence, what is the role of the manager?

OUTCOMES

The most fundamental challenge of any firm is how to be a respected business partner within its desired cluster. In order to be effective, the firm has to simultaneously compete in these **four markets**:

- Customers
- People (talent)
- Business partners, and
- Money

1. **Customers** – In order to win customers' hearts, your firm must bring them the right combination of **utility** and **cost structure**. This is a rather dynamic struggle: adapt, adopt, adapt, and adopt; a continuous dynamic process.

2. **People** – You need the right **internal business partners** (DO NOT call them employees) to effectively deal with the day-to-day tasks, while at the same time **creating the future** of the firm. This is not easy and not straightforward.

3. **Business partners** - You need the right **external business partners** to collaboratively bring the entire cluster its edge in order to compete successfully in the business sphere as a whole.

4. **Money** – If you have decent success in the previous three markets, the money markets will compensate you both in volume and in price.

This description sounds nice, doesn't it? But the BIG question is HOW?

The answer is simple to say, but very difficult to execute:

"Prompt and comprehensive response."

A prompt and comprehensive response in each market, at each decision level. That's the way to do it!

A prompt and comprehensive response in each market, at each decision level

---

I argue that this is **The Enigma**.

The Paradigm we already started to explore in Chapter Seven is how to bring the decision-making power right to where it's needed. Here, we arrive at the role of the manager.

THE ROLE OF THE MANAGER

In the eyes of "regular" managers, this will create havoc for the organization.

The main argument in Chapter Seven was the exact difference between Management 1.0 and Management 2.0.

In Management 1.0, the authority to make decisions is pushed up to the top of the organization, and hence, creates a bottleneck in decision-making.
The prompt response loses ground here.

In Management 1.0, the authority to make decisions is pushed up to the top of the organization

In Management 2.0, you give authority to make decisions right where it's needed

---

In Management 2.0, you give authority to make decisions right where it's needed.
You fully understand that the right people are close to the appropriate market, and have a better picture of what's needed.
The good manager's fears of Management 2.0 will change to accept that the new decisionmakers are fully equipped with comprehensive understanding and a good sense of responsibility.
Why? Because they have a great deal of **sense of ownership**.
Why? Because you **measure** them **correctly, compensate** them **accordingly**, and the outcome is obvious: they feel it is part of **their** business, i.e., sense of ownership.
And the role of the manager is: **Manage Less. Lead more. Be the leader**.

And the role of the manager is: Manage Less. Lead more. Be the leader.

The leader's role is to create an environment for **flow**: educate, create managerial tools, and make grand priorities, processes, and the like.

The end results are easy to describe:

- ✓ **Organizational flow** of fast and effective decisions that enable the firm to compete in the marketplace.
- ✓ **Individual flow** within the human mind.
  In 1975, **Mihaly Csikszentmihalyi** published his seminal work about the meaning of **flow**. In the years that followed, he developed and added the **dimensions of creativity** and **happiness**. The implications of **flow** in the work sphere will be provided in the next book in this series.

The claim here, that the most important role of the leader is to create an organizational culture that enables **organizational flow** and **individual flow**. The managerial implications for **flow** cannot be exaggerated: firms that walk this path will outperform their peers by far. This is the principle of the **Value Creation Mindset.**

Individual flow and organizational flow are the most important ingredients of the value creation mindset

---

Let's take for example the **productivity** theme:
Governments all around the world are concerned with the decline of productivity growth. Economists are trying to bring hard data to solve it, such as investments in fixed assets, investments in research and development, and the like.

The Value Creation Mindset takes another avenue: by measuring correctly, compensating accordingly, and managing *less*, you create a new organizational culture of sense of ownership. This will create the desired **flow**: both organizationally and at the individual level.

The value of the firm is hiding in the wrong organizational culture: Management 1.0. Management 2.0 translates into a new culture that exposes the hidden value of the firm.

THE VALUE CREATION CONCEPT

The managerial approach described this book is very simple: be short and straightforward. The nature of this managerial approach is to turn the answer upside down by starting with the solution. We are not starting with managerial concepts. We think that the overall framework leads to the right managerial concepts.
To repeat again, if you **measure correct**ly and **compensate correctly**, you will **manage less. Less is more** in term of effectiveness for any organization.

MEASURE CORRECTLY

In his book *Management Challenges for the 21st Century*, Peter F. Drucker wrote how badly we need a new measurement system. This system should measure the economics of the organization, rather than accounting criteria. There is an ocean of difference between these two approaches. In Part Two we discussed this at length.
Suppose we have an ideal system that truly **reflects** the **economics** of the organization. It will give managers the right economic perspective of past activities.

System that truly reflects the economics of the organization

It will enable managers to look forward equipped with a past understanding of the economics of their firm, and reflect it forward after making educated assumptions about the future. Of course, foresight is not perfect, but it should serve as a best guess based on realistic assumptions.

Furthermore, the measurements of future activities, the forecast if you will, should be in the same currency as past measurements. This enables managers to compare between their assumptions and actual performance.

Again, suppose this measurement system works holistically, comprehensively and simply. It has the capability to drill down to any segment required by the managers. The managers become accountable to their initiatives.

COMPENSATE CORRECTLY

Now, suppose we have a compensation system that truly reflects the economics of the firm and pays the entire workforce, from the CEO to the laypeople, fairly.

Compensation system that truly reflects the economics of the firm

---

Fairly in terms of one's (we prefer teams') contribution to the long-term economics of the firm. What do we gain? Simple: we gain the

sense of ownership. We transform the entire workforce into real business partners. All of the sudden, our big organization that suffered from too many lines of reporting, formal processes, and command and control procedures becomes a bunch of teams; each with the potential to act as one small unit, as in an early stage startup.

Good compensation system create sense of ownership

MANAGE LESS

What you see is what you get, no need for lengthy processes. The owners, the board, senior staff, and middle management work in concert. Why? They trust that the "others" are doing their very best to work as well as possible. Why? Simply because they work and act as owners. Owners are always in the position to be as effective and efficient as possible, right?

This concept sounds ideal, but there is one tiny obstacle: leading this transformation holistically and simultaneously companywide.

Work and act as owners

This takes real leadership. Leadership that understands that the people around them MUST be better than them. Leadership that understands that their team has more information, more tacit knowledge, and more expertise in making it happen.

We need leadership that understands that their team has more information, more tacit knowledge, and more expertise in making it happen

This means that leadership's role is not to work with them as like laypeople, but to give them the right tools and strategic views that will enable them to do their best. Think about Michael Jordan, Larry Bird, and other truly great athletes. These types of people were stars, but their real expertise was in developing and harvesting the potential of the people around them.

Typically, leaders do understand that this is the right way. However, they lack the tools to actualize it. They argue that the organization will slip out of their hands, and "somebody should be in charge." This is true. The fear of senior managers is real and easily justified. Our remedy is to **transform** the entire **workforce** into **business partners** that share in both successes and failures.

Transform the entire workforce into business partners that share in both successes and failures

This means each team tries to maximize its economic position for the long run. The role of senior managers should be to strike a balance between the present and the long-term, and to look for synergies between activities and teams alike.

This approach is not in contradiction to Management 2.0. On the contrary, it is a reinforcement of the Management 2.0 approach.

The difference in your journey **From Enigma to Paradigm** is the way we look at problems and how we provide the right tools to solve them.

Any good strategy needs concrete procedure, hence, the confidence of the crowd subscribing to it. If you cannot gain the trust of the crowd, it is likely to be **just**, but not **smart**. Our mothers used to tell us quite frequently that when you have obstacles, you must be smart and just. Hence, take into account everyone's best interests. Here, we face the same phenomenon: Management 2.0 is certainly very appealing. The question is how to implement it.

We think it is the same allegory that faced Columbus: how to position an egg on a flat surface. But here, we put the egg upside down. Do not go the regular course in management methodologies, start from the management itself. It's crucial to form the right behavioral framework, then all the rest will follow. In order to construct the right behavior, you have to put the egg upside down and make a crack.

The **first course** of action is the **measurement system**, to which is added the **dressing** of the **compensation system.** With these you gain the **sense of ownership** that is the **main course**, and it will appear almost naturally. Here, you might want to season it a bit, but the perfect approach of **Less is More** will lead to the most effective management on earth. This is a long and creative process, challenging and fascinating. All the stakeholders on this journey will enjoy it. The **organizational flow** and the **individual flow** will be felt throughout your firm.

It will feel like a jam session in jazz: uniquely gifted musicians playing together in flow mode. The economic outcome will follow.

CHAPTER NINE:

TOOLS & PRACTICES

This chapter is dedicated to managerial tools and practices that will help you on your journey From Enigma to Paradigm: how to make the strategic Value Creation Framework actionable.

It is not going to be an easy journey. Rather, many orthodox concepts and practices will necessarily be reevaluated along the way. You can find a few unorthodox frameworks, practices, and tools in this chapter:

1. Organization framework
2. Measurement framework
3. Remuneration practices
4. Managerial practices

ORGANIZATION FRAMEWORK

Unlike a regular organization chart, I would like to elaborate from an environmental perspective. This is my version of the **Cynefin Framework** created by David John Snowden. The essence of the Cynefin Framework is to assist managers to make sense of what they observe. For example. When you look at any object, you "see" the light that is reflected by the object. Your mind is well equipped to make sense of what you are seeing. If you are a musician, you make sense of musical notes. If you are an orthopedic doctor, you can make sense of X-rays. A manager must make sense of what she is observing.

Manager must make sense of what she is observing

In order to "make sense" you have to develop your capabilities to distinguish between:

- ✓ Noise and signals
- ✓ "Seeing" and "noticing"

Further explorations will be done in the next book of this series.

"Noise" and "signals"; "Seeing" and "noticing"

The following figures shed some light on three use cases of the Cynefin Framework, embodied by three environments within your organization.

Look at Figure 9-1:

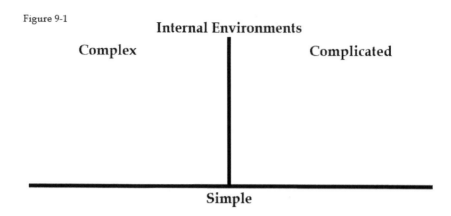

Figure 9-1

SIMPLE ENVIRONMENT

"Known Knowns" – you know that you know

Characteristics:

- A stable environment where the relationships between cause and effect are well known to almost everybody.
- Most of the time, the Simple environment is in charge of execution, and hence, generates operational cash flow.

Business sectors:

- Operations
- Human Resources (the personnel aspects)
- Accounting, and the like

Managerial positions:

- Operations, Human Resources, Logistics, and the like

Managerial aspects:

- Easy to manage day-to-day efforts.
- Narrow flexibility in workforce decisions

COMPLICATED ENVIRONMENT

"Known Unknowns" – You know that you don't know

Characteristics:

- There is no knowledge between cause and effect.
- One must investigate it by asking experts to undertake research (engineers, PhDs, Economists, Data Experts, and the like).
- You can think of similarities, and reason from one example to similar examples.
- It is a huge opportunity to learn.

Business sectors:

- Technology
- Engineering
- Economics of the firm
- Sales (definition: supply the demand)

Managerial positions:

- Technology and engineering
- Economics and Finance
- Human Resources as a business partner
- IT professionals
- Sales

Managerial aspects:

- "Think, discuss, learn and only then, act"
- For any dilemma, find the best candidate who will find the real causal relationship.
- Once you find the causal relationship, it should be robust and able to be delivered downstairs to the "Simple environment."
- Utilize and monetize your findings.

COMPLEX ENVIRONMENT

"Unknown Unknowns" – You don't know that you don't know

Since Complex environments are messy and difficult to comprehend, I will use some artillery supplied by Professor John Kay.

In his book, Kay develops the "indirectness" approach by using the word obliquity, meaning we best achieve our goals indirectly.[12] Mr. Kay elaborates:

---

[12] *Obliquity: Why Our Goals Are Best Achieved Indirectly*

Mostly, we solve problems obliquely. Our approaches are iterative and adaptive. We make our choices from a limited range of options. Our knowledge of the relevant information and of what information is relevant, is imperfect. Different people will make different judgments in the same situation, not just because they have different objectives, but because they observe different options, select different information, and assess that information differently: and even with hindsight it will often not be possible to say who was right and who was wrong. In a necessarily uncertain world, a good decision doesn't necessarily lead to a good outcome, and a good outcome doesn't necessarily imply a good decision, or a capable decision maker. The notion of a best solution may itself be misconceived.[13]

Mr. Kay sums up the major differences between directly acting on our goals versus obliquely acting on our goals:

<u>Direct action</u>
- Objectives are clear.
- Systems are comprehensible.
- We know the available options.
- What happens happens because someone intended it.
- Rules can define the system.
- Direction provides order.
- Good decisions are the product of good processes.

<u>Obliquely does it</u>

---

[13] https://www.independent.co.uk/arts-entertainment/books/features/think-oblique-how-our-goals-are-best-reached-indirectly-1922948.html

- ➢ We learn about our objectives as we strive for them.
- ➢ Systems are complex and depend on unpredictable reactions.
- ➢ We can consider only a few possibilities.
- ➢ There is no clear link between intention and outcome.
- ➢ Expertise is required, tacit knowledge is essential.
- ➢ Order often emerges and is achieved spontaneously.
- ➢ Good decisions are the product of good judgment.

I think that Mr. Kay's observations illuminate the way we have to deal with Complex environments.

Characteristics:

- There is no knowledge between cause and effect.
- Once the "expert" finds the causal relationship, make sure you fully grasp that it is **fragile** and **episodic**. It is robust for now only.
- You cannot and must not extrapolate the reasoning from this relationship into even a semblance of a relationship. Period.

Business sectors:

- Top-level management
- Business development
- Marketing (definition: identify and create demand)
  - o New markets
  - o New services for current and future clusters
- Research & development
  - o New technologies
  - o New product lines

- o New types of application engineering (alongside marketing)
- Business consultation:
  - o Strategic consultation
  - o Organization consultation

Managerial positions:

- Top-level management
- Business Development Director
- Marketing Director
- Research and Development Director
- Big Data expert
- Talent officer

Managerial aspects:

- "Think, discuss, learn, and act rapidly."
- Study fast and make small experiments.
  - o If they work, then act immediately.
  - o If they do not work, set them aside and go to the next experiment.
  - o Learn the right lessons from failures: be flexible, change the way you think, do not fall in love with your nice theories and arguments.
  - o To sum it up, adopt the appropriate attitude for a Complex environment.

Behavioral aspects:

- Humble
- Fast
- Flexible

- Share ideas
- Teammate
- Counterintuitive thinking

Figure 9-2 describes the functions that could be included in each environment:

Figure 9-2

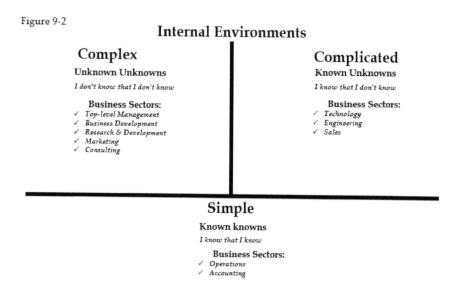

Internal Environments

Complex
Unknown Unknowns
I don't know that I don't know

Business Sectors:
✓ Top-level Management
✓ Business Development
✓ Research & Development
✓ Marketing
✓ Consulting

Complicated
Known Unknowns
I know that I don't know

Business Sectors:
✓ Technology
✓ Engineering
✓ Sales

Simple
Known knowns
I know that I know

Business Sectors:
✓ Operations
✓ Accounting

Figure 9-3 gives a few illustrations of managerial and behavioral aspects:

Figure 9-3

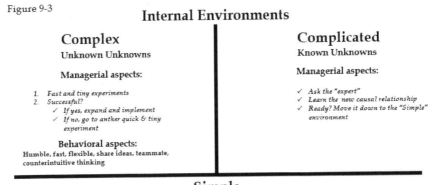

In summary, this type of organizational chart gives respect to the characteristics of the internal environment. The internal environment, not hierarchy, will dictate its own management.

The internal environment, not hierarchy, will dictate its own management

---

While you take this **internal environment framework** further to **measure, compensate,** and dictate **managerial practices**, I think you will find this organizational chart much more effective for your needs.

MEASUREMENT FRAMEWORK

The measurement system should follow two principles:

1. The economic system we developed in Part Two.
2. Internal environment aspects

THE ECONOMIC SYSTEM

First, a reminder: the major differences between the **accounting system** and the **economic system** is that they are for different purposes.

The accounting system works within tight restrictions. It must meet regulations set down by local and international authorities. It should serve an external audience such as shareholders and governments.

The economic system should serve only the decision makers: the people who create value by making the right decisions. Furthermore, it should keep confidential knowledge far from the competitors. Examples include cost structure, investment policies, and initiatives. Hence, the economic system should be constructed as a vehicle for **decision making,** to understand matters such as cost structure and prices for decision makers.

Further discussion can be found back in Part Two, but to refresh your memory, these are the major differences:

1. Opportunity costs
2. Intangibles
3. Capital employed
4. Risks of doing business

INTERNAL ENVIRONMENT ASPECTS

Simple environments take care of **Operation Strategies** (OS).

The major efforts of the **Complicated environment** take care of **Operation Strategies**. Only revolutionary efforts deal with **Growth Strategies** (GS) that can be extrapolated to create new growth engines.

The **Complex environment** is solely dedicated to **Growth Strategies**: its aim is to take care of the **future** of your company. Hence, the measurement system and the remuneration system should be completely different from the Simple Environment.

Because the measurement systems only should serve decision makers, we should deal with each internal environment separately:

1. **Simple** environment
2. **Complicated** environment
3. **Complex** environment

SIMPLE ENVIRONMENT AND THE MEASUREMENT SYSTEM

Since the Simple environment is in charge of execution (Operation Strategies), and therefore the day to day operation, the measurement system should look to **efficiency** (ratios of output to inputs) measures. Ratio measures help to benchmark and set targets for improvement.

In Figure 5-1 you will find an illustration for the operation and sales segments. We start from the overall aim of the company: ROCE > cost of capital.

This is the way a company creates value: the **Return on Capital Employed** is greater than the **risk of doing business** within a **specific industry**.

Hence, our aim is to increase the **ROCE** above the **Required Rate of Return**.

Let's take another look at the components of ROCE that serve the Simple environment. We will start with the equation:

ROCE   =   Operation Profit / Capital Employed

With algebra we can widen it to these components. Notice that the "Sales" on both sides can be eliminated, hence, the equation remains the same.

Operation Profit / Sales x Sales / Capital Employed

Now, let's dive into the basic components. We'll call them value drivers:

Figure 5-1 gives an initial illustration for breaking the ROCE into meaningful value drivers. You may want to make it more relevant to your "Simple" environment (Operations, Sales) at your particular firm. Remember, it should relate to one product line. Do not go for average calculations. Remain specific, as we discussed in the Competitive Advantage Map.

If this sounds familiar to you, then I must admit that your memory is good. In Chapter Six we discussed this in almost the same manner while dealing with corporate finance aspects of the Value Creation Concept.

Figure 5-1

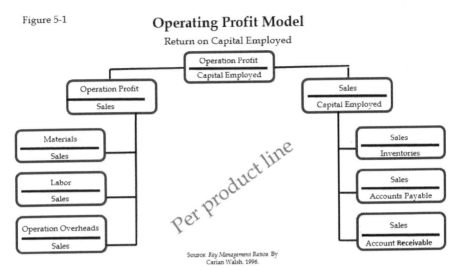

Operating Profit Model

Return on Capital Employed

Source: *Key Management Ratios.* By Carian Walsh. 1996.

COMPLICATED ENVIRONMENT AND THE MEASUREMENT SYSTEM

The Complicated environment deals with missions that need exploration and research. Hence, you are going to ask for effectiveness more than efficiency.

Effectiveness = The end result in terms of the initial expectation.

Efficiency = The ratio between output and input.

Examples:

✓ TTM = Time to Market of a new item (product, service, or technology).
✓ Dramatic reduction in cost structure due to technology change.

Most work done within the Complicated environment should improve your positioning in the marketplace, aka your competitive advantage, resulting in a new stream of operational cashflow.

Therefore, you have to set the targets in terms of value creation for your cluster and for your firm, timeline, and budget.

In my opinion, the most important targets are related to the value created for the cluster and your firm, and your timeline. You can come with the greatest solution but miss the timing, and the project goes south.

COMPLEX ENVIRONMENT AND THE MEASUREMENT SYSTEM

Due to the fact that the Complex environment is responsible for the future of the company, extreme care should be taken on setting a measurement system. Famously, the idiom that "what is not measured is not managed" is wrong.

The Complex environment cannot be measured the way Operations people are measured.

The Complex environment cannot be measured the way Operations people are measured

---

The mindset is much more like evaluating investment criteria than the mindset of an accountant, for instance. We must bear in mind that the Complex environment is responsible for new **growth engines**. Hence, much creativity should be practiced to create a new future for the company that is not ruined by the wrong measurement system.

A few examples of growth engines: new technologies, new product lines, new business models, new markets.

In each, we have to measure the end results after long periods of time, e.g. 12 - 36 months. Therefore, one cannot expect to see substantial results in the short-term. However, the company should expect new streams of operational cash flow from the new growth engines.

The idea is to prepare for each initiative a comprehensive business plan. The measurement system should be applied as any other business plan. In Chapter Six we dealt with this briefly. Go back and take a look at the subject of strategic investment.

REMUNERATION PRACTICES

Remuneration practices are part of the management of a firm. They should support the **sense of ownership** and go hand-in-hand with the measurement system.

In the **Simple environment**, we want to use the value drivers that support the overall ROCE measures. A sense of ownership can be derived by measuring only the change in each value driver, not absolute numbers. This is very important. Absolute measures encourage manipulation and gaming the system. We would like to see that each value driver is improving constantly.

You will be amazed with the creativity a team will use to improve. The trick is to use benchmarking within your industry. If you cannot, then measure annually. Compensating in cash bonuses will encourage the right attitude and behavior.

In the **Complicated environment**, you should compensate only on real new improvement for each initiative, i.e. a new stream of operational cash flow. The measurement system should be equipped with "memory" to make sure that it reflects each new stream of operational cash flow from each new initiative.

This will boost the **sense of ownership** and will motivate teams in the right direction and reward appropriate behavior.

In **Complex environments**, we need to be creative. The entire essence of compensation is to have it NOW. Since we are dealing with business development that takes a long time, I suggest putting money at risk: create a "bonus bank" that reflects the magnitude of success derived from each initiative.

If there is success, the bonus bank will transform into cash bonuses. If the initiative is a failure, the bonus bank will evaporate.

We must take into consideration that the Complex environment invites many failures. We, as human beings, do not like failures. Furthermore, subordinates fear that failure will ruin their future in the firm. Any innovation program needs to support failure and how to learn from it. Our prescription for the Complex environment is to encourage many tiny tests to see what will work and what will not work.

Hence, we need another approach. I think the seminal work done by **Raghuram Ragan** et al. about **internal governance** gives good direction (*The Internal Governance of Firms.* 2010). Their idea is to tie the long-term compensation of the CEO to people who report to her. Connecting long term goals in areas such as R&D, business development, and marketing ensures the CEO and his team are investing in the future of the firm, even if it hurts short-term goals like the quarterly and annual profit & loss statements.
A rough example would be to dedicate a substantial portion of the CEO's compensation to the long-term goals of R&D.
He would be a beneficiary due to the success of R&D projects, even after he left the firm. This principle can be rolled out to the entire membership of the Complex environment: directors, teams, and collaborators.

Here, I equip you with a few ideas that you can implement in your own way. Any regular option plan can do the job just as well, but I argue that teams would like to have a better line of sight and influence with their achievements. And, as a result, it's much more effective in terms of end results.

In the next book, I will bring on board a comprehensive framework for the two environments: Complicated and Complex. It will be eye opening for many people.

MANAGERIAL PRACTICES

The major theme of this book can be summarized as follows:

In order to compete successfully, the firm must treat opportunities and threats appropriately and quickly. Very quickly. This can be done only if you delegate responsibilities to the places where the decisions must take place: where people know best. In order to not lose control, you must hold them accountable for their decisions. By measuring them correctly and compensating them appropriately, you give them the appropriate sense of ownership. Then, you can manage… less.

If you succeed in building this type of management architecture and atmosphere, your chances to win the competitive edge rise dramatically.

To delegate responsibilities to the places where the decisions must take place: where people know best.

In order to not lose control, you must hold them accountable for their decisions.

By measuring them correctly and compensating them appropriately,
you give them the appropriate sense of ownership.

Then, you can manage… less.

CHAPTER TEN:

THE HUMAN FACTOR

Final thoughts

Dear reader, well done!

We are approaching the final lap of our journey
From Enigma to Paradigm.
I would like to tell you a secret: we just studied the
knowledge required to go From Enigma to
Paradigm together. But in order to do this for real,
we need to add the most powerful ingredient, the
human dimension.

We need to add the most powerful ingredient, the human dimension

---

Let me elaborate on it from a different angle.
In culinary circles, we know that the most successful dishes require
a relationship between texture, sourness, sweetness, saltiness,
bitterness, and many other factors. On the eve of the 20th century,
Japanese scientist Professor Kikunae Ikeda discovered the fifth
taste, umami.
Umami intensifies taste by balancing the overall flavor of a dish.
I am sure you know it; you feel it: you add mature cheese to pasta
and pizza, you add ketchup to French fries, you add mushrooms,
and you like the taste of meat, poultry and fish.

Umami intensifies taste by balancing the overall flavor of a dish

---

Experts in the culinary sphere declare that without umami, our food would taste dull. They call it the **ultimate ingredient. Umami reflects the human factor of our journey.**

This analogy can serve us managers well, but in a more powerful way. When we do not take into account the human factor, we drastically decrease the effectiveness of managerial work.
So, in this chapter, I brief you on the human dimension. Further explorations will be done in the next book of this series.
Some call it "**corporate culture,**" others call it the **DNA** of an organization. Then came all the buzz about **human capital** and **social capital**. I will draw a picture that is easy to comprehend and actionable for you; **building blocks** for the **architecture** of the **business** and **human culture** of your **organization.**
Here is a glimpse of these building blocks.

MUTUAL TRUST AND RESPECT

Professor Ichak Adizes is the most powerful advocate of **mutual trust and respect** (MTR). He claims that the energy required to manage organizations effectively is the result of MTR.
Managing organizations that are characterized by a diverse workforce makes MTR more challenging on the one hand, and yet that much more necessary on the other hand.
Trust is feeling that your colleagues' intentions for the organization as a whole, and for you in particular, are good.

Respect is when you are aware that your colleagues' arguments have grounds and legitimacy, even when you disagree.

Mutual trust and respect are achieved when you first "give" the trust and respect. Then you "get" it.

It is a process. Hard to build step-by-step, and easy to destroy with one stupid confrontation. Remember, you don't have to win all the "battles." Ego out. Any debate can be a source of growth and learning.

Trust is feeling that your colleagues' intentions for the organization as a whole, and for you in particular, are good.

Respect is when you are aware that your colleagues' arguments have grounds and legitimacy, even when you disagree.

Hence, mutual trust and respect is one of the building blocks of our journey From Enigma to Paradigm.

MENSCH

Dear manager, I would like you to be a mensch. I would like you to raise the bar and inspire your colleagues to be mensches. *Mensch*, in German, means human being, "a person of integrity and honor".[14] According to Leo Rosten, the Yiddish maven and author of *The Joys of Yiddish*, a mensch is "someone to admire and emulate, someone of noble character. The key to being "a real mensch is nothing less

---

14 https://www.merriam-webster.com/dictionary/mensch

than character, rectitude, dignity, a sense of what is right, responsible, decorous." The term is used as a high compliment, implying the rarity and value of that individual's qualities[15]
In other words, you may want to follow the **Golden Rule** that appears in many religious texts: **treat others as you would like others to treat you**[16] Period. This is how you earn the **desired mutual trust and respect**. It will inject positive energy into your organization and make your journey From Enigma to Paradigm much more effective and enjoyable.

Mensch means human being, "person of integrity and honor"

HUMAN CAPITAL

If you have been following this book, you've sensed that I don't like the mumbo jumbo around the human capital phenomenon. You are right. I'd rather stir the discussion to other avenues.
As you may have already guessed, human capital does not refer to one guru or one extraordinarily gifted person. Nowadays, everything is teamwork. Nothing can be done by a single person, no matter how talented they are.
For me, human capital is all about working with people I admire personally and professionally. People that are curious and knowledgeable, but humble; people who fit their work's challenges but have the desire and capability to rise to new opportunities.

---

15 : https://en.wikipedia.org/wiki/Mensch
16 https://en.wikipedia.org/wiki/Golden_Rule

People who like to work in teams and share information. People with a sense of personal accountability, ego out. People that connect to their minds and hearts while working together. People who feel a sense of ownership.

From my standpoint, these types of people can be characterized as human capital. Human capital at its smallest unit: one human being.

People that connect to their minds and hearts while working together. People who feel a sense of ownership

---

But this is not enough. You, as the manager, should provide the "glue" for the human capital. The "glue" is the social capital: how all of these marvelous people work together. Others might call it corporate culture, corporate DNA, and the like.

The manager, should provide the "glue" for the human capital. The "glue" is the social capital

---

EMOTIONAL INTELLIGENCE (EI)

In order to successfully participate in the dynamics I described earlier, one has to have a high degree of **Emotional Intelligence**. Millions of words have been written to analyze this desirable quality. I am not going to enter this wild arena. Instead, I will give you a quick glimpse to enable you to use your own **Emotional Intelligence** (EI) in a more intuitive way:

EI is "the **awareness** of your own and other people's **emotions** and the **ability** to use this information to **guide** your **thinking** and **behavior**."[17]

Use Emotional Intelligence to guide your thinking and behavior

---

Daniel Goleman invested time and effort into making EI easy to grasp. The real problem with EI is that it is about emotion. Your **mind** cannot always dictate how to **feel** or how to **react**. Hence, fully understanding EI is a lifetime project. Ideally, you can struggle through with your closest friends who can comfortably confront you and help you discover ways to "nudge" your behaviors.

Let me be much clearer: the bad news is that you cannot study EI. The good news is that you become better as you age.

You cannot be an expert in EI, nor can you teach others. Reading books and articles can give you an overall understanding of EI, but this type of understanding is just the first step in the journey to become a better manager; to become a person who is aware of their own emotions, others' emotions, and how to navigate the ship of human relations in a better way. In my experience with different types of people, it can be practiced in small groups with the right guidance. Let's dive into the matter.

Daniel Goleman[18] divided EI into five main components:

	Definition	Hallmarks
Self-awareness	The ability to recognize and understand your moods, emotions, and drives, as well as	Self-confidence

	their effect on others	Realistic self-assessment Self-deprecating sense of humor
Self-regulation	The ability to control or redirect disruptive impulses and moods The propensity to suspend judgment, to think before acting	Trustworthiness and integrity Comfort with ambiguity Openness to change
Motivation	A passion to work for reasons that go beyond money and status A propensity to pursue goals with energy and persistence	Strong drive to achieve optimism, even in the face of failure Organizational commitment
Empathy	The ability to understand the emotional makeup of other people Skill in treating people according to their emotional reactions	Expertise in building and retaining talent Cross-cultural sensitivity Service to clients and customers
Social skill	Proficiency in managing relationships and building networks An ability to find common ground and build rapport	Effectiveness in leading change Persuasiveness Expertise in building and leading teams

---

[17] FT – September 2014.
[18] "What Makes a Leader", by Daniel Goleman, HBR November-December 1998

My approach to improving the EI of executive groups is as follows: A working group session. The atmosphere should be relaxed. Beer is not just allowed, it is essential. Steps:

1. Let the group thoroughly read the chart above.
2. Reread and explain each component and give real examples from your own life. This will prepare the group for their own pitches.
3. Tell each group member to raise one example of each of the five components. It should be an example of success or failure. They should elaborate on it at length.
4. These sessions will replay in the minds of the participants for a long time.

My advice is to do it once a month for six months. My guess is that it will change the interrelations of the group for the better.

INTERNAL BROKER

Forget the image of a middleman in the Market. The concept of a broker was developed to better describe the intangibles that create value in strategic matters.

Let's take a look at the broker phenomenon:

Do you know people in your organization who spend too much time around the coffee machine gossiping?

Do you know people that seemingly do nothing except reaching out to other people within the organization?

These sorts of people have bad reputations for missing deadlines.

Sometimes managers identify them as "rotten apples" that must be removed. Why? Because if you have one rotten apple in a box, if you don't remove it immediately, all of the apples become rotten. Only rare managers have the intellectual power to recognize the importance of these types of people through the fog of rumors and reputation.

Let me suggest that you think differently. These types of people can be identified as **internal brokers**.

They break the organizational structure and seek information and knowledge about the organization that no one else has. Mostly **intangible knowledge** that cannot be obtained and documented. Let's be clear: an internal broker with bad intent is a rotten apple and should be removed.

An internal broker with good intent is the most valuable asset within the organization, period.

Why? **Organizational knowledge** is rare. You cannot Google it and you cannot gain it from a sophisticated survey or by any other means.

Organizational knowledge is the deep and thorough understanding of what is really happening in the organization, what people really know, and what unstructured networking is taking place in real time.

To sum it up, what senior people should know and understand, but have no quality time to figure out. The internal broker has a deep understanding of what is really going on. S/he knows where to seek valuable information. S/he knows who the people that hold valuable knowledge are. To put it simply, you want to have good **internal brokers** around you.

The internal broker has a deep understanding of what is really going on

The bright manager develops informal relationship with such people, asking them to participate in meetings un-related to their job description, and consulting them when reaching organizational turning points.

These internal brokers are the perfect embodiment of combining of human capital with social capital.

Unfortunately, internal brokers gain bad reputations in the first place because they tend to be unproductive and to pour gasoline on the flames, so to speak. To manage them, the bright manager contains criticism and bad behavior. But in the end, the bright manager earns an intangible and unique type of **social capital**: amazing quantity and quality relationships within the organization.

Ronald S. Burt put it this way, "Where **relationships bridge structural holes,** people are more likely to encounter **new ideas, create good ideas,** as well as **express, discuss, and see how to implement ideas**[19]

The following sentence beautifully describes the hidden capabilities of both internal and external brokers:

"Two factors define courses of action: **data** and **colleagues.**
- ✓ The **data are what you know.**
- ✓ The **colleagues are who you know.**"[20]

---

[19] "Brokerage & Closure. An Introduction to Social Capital" page 59, Ronald S. Burt. 2005
[20] "Brokerage & Closure. An Introduction to Social Capital" page 94, Ronald S. Burt. 2005

Ronald S. Burt is one of the pioneers of explaining social capital in more practical ways. You can feel the echo of his work throughout this book.

EXTERNAL BROKER

Think about internal brokers, and aim them outside: people that "live" on the edge of your organization and have a huge amount of relationships outside. Some examples include people in procurement, marketing, sales, technology, business development, as well as external consultants, advisers, and others.
External brokers gain knowledge about the intersections of your organization and specific external domains. Earlier, we called these external domains "clusters" of your ecosystem.

The external broker knows how your organization intersects with external domains

---

Administrative entities like Finance and HR sometimes limit opportunities for formal and informal meetings due to budget constraints and other weak arguments. Nobody can calculate the immediate results of attending conferences or meeting with professionals. There is no way to calculate the immediate ROI. These types of contacts should be developed, and one should develop relationships with these types of people. It is one of the most important intangibles of an organization. And, if you really believe in **building distinctive capabilities**, this is the place.

I promise, when your company faces strategic turning points, these are the people you want around you.

SOCIAL CAPITAL

Please recall your experience with social capital. It will give you ideas for how to increase the social capital within your organization.

Generally speaking, social capital is the "**invisible glue**" that conveys trust, norms, and coordination. Hence, it provides good ideas and practices that lead to better business performance.

Social capital is the "invisible glue" that conveys trust, norms, and coordination

---

"Almost everything that happens in a firm **flows** through **informal networks** built by **advice, coordination, cooperation, friendship, gossip, knowledge, and trust.**"[21]

Ronald S. Burt gives his outlook on the meaning of social capital: "Social capital is the contextual complement to human capital in explaining advantage.

Social capital explains how people do better because they are somehow better connected with other people…trusting certain others, obligated to support certain others, dependent to exchange with certain others."[22]

---

[21] https://www.amazon.com/Brokerage-Closure-Introduction-Clarendon-Management/dp/0199249156

[22] "Brokerage & Closure. An Introduction to Social Capital" page 4, Ronald S. Burt. 2005

Coleman adds another layer, "Like other forms of capital, social capital is productive, making possible the achievement of certain ends that would not be attainable in its absence."[23]

"Social capital is the contextual complement to human capital in explaining advantage…"

"Social structure defines a kind of capital that can create for individuals or groups an advantage in pursuing their ends. People and groups who do well are somehow better connected…The issue is performance. Social capital promises to yield new insights, and a more rigorous and stable model, describing why certain people and organizations perform better than others…such as coordination, creativity, discrimination, entrepreneurship, leadership, learning, teamwork, and the like".[24]

I don't need to walk you through this further, as the social capital phenomenon encapsulates the following subjects that we've already covered:

1. Mutual Trust and Respect
2. Mensch
3. Human capital
4. Emotional Intelligence
5. Internal and external Brokers

My advice is to reread the subjects above with a better understanding of the essence of **social capital**:

✓ How to create it.
✓ Its outcomes from two perspectives:

[23] Coleman, 1998:s98, 1990: 302
[24] "Brokerage & Closure. An Introduction to Social Capital" page 5, Ronald S. Burt. 2005

1. The human perspective
2. The organizational perspective

Personal note
This chapter outlined personal characteristics and strategies that make anyone a better collaborator for the business of your firm. On this note, I like people and teams that are "round." Let me elaborate:
- ✓ **Easy to do business with** both within the organization and externally.
- ✓ **Easy to exchange counterintuitive thoughts and insights with**.

This type of **ease** creates **uniqueness: human capital** and **social capital atmosphere.**
Furthermore, it will enable you to seek the competitive edge that you need so desperately to create value for all of your stakeholders.

FINAL REMARKS

In this book, I have done my best to equip you, my reader, with useful insights and practices that make you more capable of coping with our turbulent business world.
I started with these questions:
- ✓ How many times were you bothered by the direction your company is taking?
- ✓ How many times have you heard mumbo jumbo corporate strategy?

✓ How many times have consultants spewed jargon on how to steer your company, and you didn't have a clue what to do next?

This was the start of our journey **From Enigma to Paradigm**.

Our journey was dedicated to the best practices of **management-in-action.**

We treated three separated domains as one entity:

4. **Strategy**

   How your company can measure its **competitive advantage** in three dimensions: technology, brand, and finance.

5. **Finance**

   How your company can create **shareholder value** by taking its **stakeholders** into account.

6. **Management**

How to make it all happen.

I hope you found your journey From Enigma to Paradigm worthwhile, both financially and in terms of your valuable time.

You are more than welcome to share ideas and insights with me. You can be sure that I will incorporate the relevant ones into the next edition of this book, with your contribution cited.

Since this is the first book in a series, you may find them in the upcoming volumes.

Sincerely yours,
Amnon Danzig

www.amnondanzig.com
amnon.danzig@gmail.com

Amnon Danzig

FURTHER READING, INSTEAD OF ACKNOWLEDGMENTS

Closing Notes

This is not an academic text, therefore I am not obliged to follow the source and citation conventions by which the academic world is bound.
This is a book for managers in the SME area of manufacturing. Managers who work in firms with multi-division framework will benefit as well.

Why?

Because, in the end, competitive advantage is not always on a large scale. It is applicable to all businesses that have a specific marketing niche.

Ordinary people like me do not write books because they want to. I wrote this book because I felt that I must, that I had a contribution to make to the way managers go about their work. Here, I have to thank Professor Oded Sarig, who encouraged me to do so. I did not understand his claim, "You are going to learn a lot while writing the book." I thought I was well prepared...but, while writing it, I was astonished by the wealth of knowledge and insights to which I have been exposed to over the last 30 years. Learning become a daily routine after repeated exposure to my inner voice.

What's the meaning of inner voice?
Over the last three decades, I've read many books from a broad spectrum of fields, and worked with many people around the globe. At the time, I was not consciously aware of what I was gaining from all these texts and colleagues. In hindsight, though, it all combined to become my inner voice.

While writing this book, I "heard" this voice like an echo, instructing me along the way. It is my pleasure to give you a glimpse into the sources that molded and enriched my thinking. For each source, I will explain why you should read it.

First, a word about reading. I am afraid that busy managers do not read enough. They are too preoccupied, or the text just isn't engaging enough. Let me share with you the reasons why you should read more.

Reading is an intellectual effort. If you read a wide variety of subjects, you develop an augmented reality within your mind that develops your own creativity and capabilities to innovative. Let me explain: the intersection of ideas, concepts, and insights that you develop while reading is the springboard for the way you observe and conceptualize the complex environments you live and work in.

Managers who read across a variety of fields claim they are given a unique opportunity to have an intimate "chat" with a smart person whom they would otherwise never "meet." It provides in-depth knowledge from multiple perspectives. It increases your curiosity and reason methods. It makes you more aware that life is not simple, and that there is no "good" or "bad." Hence, there are not any black and white solutions. It will enrich your vocabulary professionally and personally. It will give you many opportunities to discuss topics with colleagues who will admire your knowledge, which is, essentially, your reputation.

While reading, you will have an inner debate that encourages the generation of new ideas. And it will become part of your thinking that you'll carry forward. This is exactly what happened to me while writing this book.

The List
So, here is a glimpse of what influenced me, in no particular order. It's organized by intuition.

1. The EVA Challenge. Joel M. Stern and John S. Shiely

Joel has been my long-term mentor without even knowing it. His contribution to the way I think and work is far beyond my consciousness. This book beautifully elaborates how a well-known firm implemented the EVA concept. There are many insights you can gain here.

2. **The Value Mindset. Erik Stern and Mike Hutchinson.**

   Erik is my long-term colleague, with one of the most creative minds I've ever met. In this book, he explores different industries and internal environments. It's worthwhile to explore whether you are facing the same dilemmas mentioned in this book.

3. **The Quest for Value. C. Bennett Stewart,** III

   If you are looking for the mechanics of EVA framework, this is a good place to start.

4. **Valuation: Measuring and Managing the Value of Companies. Tim Koller, Marc Goedhart and David Wessels.**

   Tim Koller worked with Stern Stewart & Co. This is a heavy book (sometimes too heavy) that equips you with insights and mechanics. Most of the time, it seems that they simply changed the terminology and definitions of the EVA framework, but the meaning remains the same.

5. **Beyond Budgeting. Jeremy Hope and Robin Fraser.**

   This is unique book that explores how to run the budgeting process in much more robustly and effectively.

6. **Beyond Performance Management. Jeremy Hope and Steve Player.**

   Tools and practices for the concept of "Beyond Budgeting."

7. **Good Strategy, Bad Strategy. Richard P. Rumelt.**

   Currently, this is my favorite book about strategy. The author presents it so that a manager can digest it quite easily.

8. **Why Firms Succeed: Choosing Markets and Challenging Competitors to Add Value. John Kay.**

This is an extremely valuable book for managers who want to connect strategy with value creation. I feel grateful to have had the opportunity to read this book many times over the past few years.

9. **Strategy Safari: The Guided Tour Through the Wilds of Strategic Management. Henry Mintzberg, Bruce Ahlstrand and Joseph Lampel.**
   Henry Mintzberg is one of the most unique contributors to modern managerial thinking. He is a counterintuitive scholar. Here, he walks you through ten schools of thought in the strategy field.

10. **Strategy Bites Back: It is Far More, and Less, Than You Ever Imagine. Henry Mintzberg, Bruce Ahlstrand, Joseph Lampel.**
    This is Henry Mintzbreg at his best: short articles from wise contributors. A must read book for rethinking strategy.

11. **Company Analysis: Determining Strategic Capability. Per Jenster and David Hussey.**
    This is a nice gateway to begin thinking strategically.

12. **Value Creation: The Definitive Guide for Business Leaders.** Gautam Mahajan
    If you really want to enter the right way to the "Value Creation" sphere, this is the first step.

13. **Implanting Strategic Management. H. Igor Ansoff.**
    Igor Ansoff is one of the pioneers of strategic thinking. His framework is robust and detailed.

14. **The Profit Zone: How Strategic Business Design Will Lead You to Tomorrow's Profits. Adrian J. Slywotzky and David J. Morrison.**
    Here, you can confront many "obvious" and non-obvious questions and be surprise by the answers.

15. **Brokerage & Closure: An Introduction to Social Capital. Ronald S. Burt.**
    A must read book on an important aspect of strategy thinking: the human factor.

16. **Beyond HR: The New Science of Human Capital. John W. Boudreau, Peter M. Ramstad.**

    Again, how the human factor influences strategy, and vice-versa.

17. **Board Perspective: Building Value Through Strategy, Risk Assessment, and Renewal. William J. Hass and Shepherd G. Pryor IV.**

    A unique perspective through the lens of a Board of Directors. Highly recommended for Directors.

18. **The Future of Management. Gary Hamel.**

    Here you will find a wealth of ideas and insights concerning new management styles and practices.

19. **Key Management Ratios: How to Analyze, Compare, and Control the Figures That Drive the Company Value. Ciaran Walsh.**

    Good starting point for understanding accounting framework.

20. **Key Management Ideas: Thinkers That Changed the Management World. Stuart Crainer.**

    An excellent handbook for discovering ideas and innovators.

21. **Managing. Henry Mintzberg.**

    Those who fall in love with Mintzberg's ideas and the way that he reflects on them must read this book.

22. **Changing Minds: The Art and Science of Changing our Own and Other People's Minds. Howard Gardner.**

    A must read book for managers who want to understand their own thinking better.

23. **The Medici Effect: Breakthrough Insights at the Intersection of Ideas, Concepts & Cultures. Frans Johansson.**

    Excellent book for managers who want to discover the innovation phenomenon.

24. **Outliers: The Story of Success. Malcolm Gladwell.**

    An extremely enjoyable read that will give you a few ideas on why you want to employ certain types of people, and what you can gain from that as a manager. You can relate to these books, as well: The Medici Effect, Peak, and Brokerage & Closure.

25. **Peak: Secrets From the New Science of Expertise. Anders Ericsson and Robert Pool.**
If you've heard of the 10,000 hours rule, Ericsson is the originator. Malcolm Gladwell has done good marketing for this rule. If you want to understand it deeper, as well as why any manager needs at least 3-4 years in a new company, you will find the answer here. If you want to understand why and how a company needs to train a "meister" (master), this is the book. (Note: A "meister" is a person whose skills are at the highest level that benefits a manufacturing firm in Germany).

26. **Thinking, Fast and Slow. Daniel Kahneman.**
A popular book about behavioral economics. An enjoyable read and an influential book for managers. Ignites your thinking about the way we think and behave.

27. **Misbehaving: The Making of Behavioral Economics. Richard H. Thaler**
Another popular book about behavioral economics. Kahneman and Thaler are very good friends who, together with Amos Tversky, pioneered this insightful new branch of economics.

28. **Against the Current. Isaiah Berlin.**
An excellent book for those who want to widen the scope of their reading. Not an easy book, but extremely valuable in introducing you to the history of ideologies. It will enrich your thinking and reasoning about new phenomena in complex environments.

29. **Personal Impressions. Isaiah Berlin.**
Here you will find inspiring articles about people who played very important roles. Like Isaiah Berlin, you will gain wise insights from such leading figures.

30. **World Order. Henry Kissinger.**
A heavy book with historic view from a leading 20th century statesman. Furthermore, Kissinger illustrates a picture for the 21st

century as well. Remember that, in the end, his view concerning processes and decisions can also be adapted to your world.

TESTIMONIALS

- *"It is ambitious in its reach but it is well done."*
- *"In a world of big data and powerful tools, we need big picture thinking more than ever before. Amnon's book, From Enigma to Paradigm, traverses and connects different business disciplines (from strategy to finance to marketing) to provide that perspective, without lapsing into buzzwords and jargon."*
Aswath Damodaran
Stern School of Business

I believe the book contains a great many good ideas for managers. Amnon has done a service for his colleagues in taking the time to produce this book.
Ronald S. Burt,
Hobart W. Williams Professor of Sociology and Strategy
University of Chicago Booth School of Business

Amnon Danzig's book is easy to read and helps you master management practices and entices you into newer thinking like value creation, intangible investments such as human and social capital making you embrace modern techniques and become winners. The magic of this book is that it makes complex issues easy to understand and use.

A must read book if you want to grow and succeed in your company.

Gautam Mahajan,
President, Customer Value Foundation and Inter-
Link India
Founder Editor, Journal of Creating
Value jcv.sagepub.com

Powerful, practical insights in a compact package!
Enigma to Paradigm combines conceptual power and practicality with refreshing brevity as Mr. Danzing outlines frameworks for innovation girded by strong business fundamentals.
Why is this important?
In an era where markets seem to keep rising, start ups are the rage (deja vu?), betting that modern day Unicorns grow to be more real than the mythical origins of the name -- we eagerly wait to see which start ups actually become viable, current stratospheric valuations or not.
Against this backdrop is a reminder that good business is built upon solid foundation.
True innovation requires brilliant, tenacious, execution – not just "powerpoints".
In parallel, Mr. Danzig guides the reader to foundations of business discipline while encouraging and celebrating business leaders to strive and forge ahead.

Entrepreneurs, corporate executives, board members and investors will benefit from this book as common touch point to assure that operation supports vision, vision supported by structure.

Not brittle but nimble to respond to expanding markets as well as economic uncertainty or downturn. Always remember that the Moonshot had very capable ground team.

Enigma to Paradigm is a very interesting book for these very interesting times.

Richard A Mandahl, MBA
Managing Director
Mandahl Associates, LLC
Salt Lake City